T0329936

THE PANDEMIC WITHIN
Policy Making for a Better World

Hendrik Wagenaar and Barbara Prainsack

First published in Great Britain in 2021 by

Policy Press, an imprint of
Bristol University Press
University of Bristol
1–9 Old Park Hill
Bristol
BS2 8BB
UK
t: +44 (0)117 954 5940
e: bup-info@bristol.ac.uk

Details of international sales and distribution partners are available at
policy.bristoluniversitypress.co.uk

British Library Cataloguing in Publication Data
A catalogue record for this book is available from the British Library

ISBN 978-1-4473-6222-7 hardcover
ISBN 978-1-4473-6223-4 paperback
ISBN 978-1-4473-6224-1 ePub
ISBN 978-1-4473-6225-8 ePdf

Cover design: Robin Hawes
Image credit: iStock/Orbon Alija
Bristol University Press and Policy Press use environmentally responsible
print partners.
Printed in Great Britain by CMP, Poole

Contents

Acknowledgements

We are indebted to a great many people, colleagues and friends with whom we have shared and discussed our ideas over the years, who have generously shared theirs and who encouraged us to pursue this project. We would like to highlight a few people whose involvement in this book has been particularly important: Anita Aigner, Julia Raptis, Roy Heidelberg and Robert Braun we thank for sharing with us their expertise on housing policy in Vienna, the finance industry, public administration and corporate social responsibility, respectively. Any mistakes are wholly ours. The Writing Group at the Department of Political Science at the University Vienna we thank for their very helpful comments on several chapters. Patsy Healey, John Boswell, Ori (Guli) Dolev-Hashiloni and the anonymous reviewers at Policy Press offered valuable suggestions for improvement of various stages of the full manuscript, for which we are particularly grateful. Linsey McGoey and Gísli Pálsson have enthusiastically supported our project from its start as a series of blogs. We thank Elias Weiss for his invaluable help as a research assistant, and Emily Watt, Caroline Astley and Laura Vickers-Rendall of Policy Press who expertly brought this book to publication.

Introduction:
The pandemic within

Occasionally, in the ongoing torrent of news and information that forms the background to our everyday lives, we are confronted with a story or image that, because it drives home the enormity of a particular situation, stops us in our tracks. The photo of 3-year-old Alan Kurdi, lying face down on the waterline of a Turkish beach, drowned on 2 September 2015, in an attempt to reach European shores, was such an image. It encapsulated the full horror of the Syrian refugee crisis that was unfolding in the Mediterranean. The image of that small lifeless body filled the viewer with emotions of pity and anger, a helpless feeling of being a bystander to a situation of vast moral complexity and unscrupulous political calculation.

Reading the first pages of Jessica Bruder's *Nomadland. Surviving America in the Twenty-First Century* (2017) prompted a similar visceral reaction in one of us (HW). In a virtuoso act of reporting, Bruder introduces a cast of characters whose lives she describes in the book. A former San Francisco cab driver, 67, who labours 12 hours a day, in sub-zero temperatures, at the annual sugar beet harvest in Minnesota. A 66-year-old former general contractor who walks 15 miles per shift in a vast Amazon warehouse in Campbellsville Kentucky. Or 64-year-old Linda May, standing in front of her tiny trailer, in the snow, in the campground where she makes 12 to 14 hour days as a camp host, receiving visitors, and cleaning toilets and camp sites. These women and men are itinerant workers who drive around the United States in search of work. Their cars, trailers or campervans are their homes. They have given up their 'sticks and bricks' house, and whatever dream they had of retiring, because they lost their job, business or 401(k) pension, and can no longer afford the monthly mortgage payments. Bruder reports how Amazon, ever pushing the frontier of corporate innovation, has created the 'Camperforce' programme to attract this itinerant population to augment its workforce during peak times, such as the months before Christmas. (This advance in human resource innovation has no doubt been facilitated by the opportunity to collect federal tax credits ranging from 25 and 40 per cent of wages, in return for hiring older workers; Bruder, 2017, 59.) They make long hours in dirty, mindless, backbreaking work. They never earn more than the hourly minimum wage, usually less. They have no pension, sick or disability pay, or job security. They are the flotsam of naked capitalism.

When I started reading *Nomadland* I was sitting in my study in our apartment in Vienna. The first cold nights of the autumn had set in and I faintly heard the central heating boiler kicking in at regular intervals. We had rented the flat, in a First World War Jugendstil building in the foothills of the Wiener Wald, in 2014, with an indefinite lease and strict rent control. Rent increases are restricted to the annual rate of inflation. As we will describe in Chapter 4, Vienna boasts a large public housing sector. We live next to one of the largest public housing estates in the city, the *Hugo Breitner Hof*, a large complex of flats in attractive 4-storey buildings situated around large, park-like courtyards. The private rental sector in Vienna is heavily regulated with tenant protection measures that go back more than a century. Viennese housing policy is aimed at providing access and security to residents. As a result, many more people rent than own their homes, and the ability to obtain high quality housing in the city is independent of the ability to pay.

The contrast between our personal situation and the unsettled, fluctuating life of these new nomads – people at retirement age, often with similar middle class lives as ours, that have been brutally interrupted by economic or other calamities – could not be more striking. I cannot begin to imagine the anguish and forlornness that sitting in their small trailer on a cold night in a Minnesota or Omaha parking lot must evoke in these 'workcampers'. Not knowing where the next job will be. Fearing a sudden injury that could threaten their existence. One catastrophic vehicle breakdown away from destitution. And although the interviews in the book showed enormous resilience and pluckiness among these workers, and many relate stories of friendship and solidarity, it was clear that all of them, at the onset of old age, had collided with the brute iniquity of the American economy.

It is a truism that the pandemic created by the SARS-CoV-2 virus has cruelly exposed the fault lines of our political-economic order, fissures such as the large drifting population of itinerant workers in the US, or the millions of rent arrears held at bay by national eviction bans.[1] In the early stages of the COVID-19 crisis this realisation was trenchantly expressed by an anonymous graffiti artist in Hong Kong: 'There can be no return to normal because normal was the problem in the first place.' (Wintour, 2020) But as with all self-evident truths, while they speak directly to the heart, they leave a lot unsaid. Few people would deny that the writing was on the wall, at least since the financial crisis of 2008. Even the plutocrats now notice 'problems around structural racism and poverty', as *The Guardian* Banking correspondent Kalyeena Makortoff (2020) summarises a speech given by JP Morgan CEO Jamie Dimon. The combination of a hyperconnected global trade system, overleveraged financial markets, and a dysfunctional political system have somehow created the circumstances that allowed the virus to hit us so hard, health-wise and economically. Yet, it is not at all clear how these fault lines emerged, what our role in it has been, and above all, why, despite clear warnings, we have been so unsuccessful in improving the situation. For example, the imminent dangers of climate catastrophe, the fragility of the global financial order, as well as extreme inequality in wealth and income, both within and between countries, were obvious and have been documented and debated over and over again. Yet our record in alleviating these acute problems has been patchy at best, even before the COVID-19 crisis.

Perhaps problem setting is a good place to start. The writing about the alarming state of the political-economic order in recent years has a somewhat repetitive quality. Often it takes the form of a depressing listing of egregious injustices, an angry diatribe against greedy and corrupt elites in finance, business and politics, or a forensic dissection of one of the many current social, moral or environmental ills. To analysts of public policy, as both of us are, consensus in problem setting is a worrisome sign. Policy theory stipulates that there are many ways to frame a problem, that problem formulation is as much shaped by ideology as by evidence, and that the formulation of the problem predestines its solution. The critical genres that we mentioned above have in common that they assume an external observer, someone who occupies an Archimedean position from which they issue their opinions and declarations. As we will show in the next chapter, that is practically impossible and heuristically misleading. As the British sociologist Bronislaw Szerszynski (2019) has argued, we are an integral part of the planetary order. The planet resonates within us as much as we put our imprint on it. We are always part of the world that we observe. That is the human predicament and, practically and morally, it is a realisation that is too big to behold in our instrumentalist universe. Instead, we position ourselves outside the world and approach nature and society in an objectified manner, instrumentally, as something to be observed dispassionately and wielded to our advantage. This is how experts and officials portray the COVID-19 pandemic, as an external enemy, an invader from distant, hostile lands, which has overtaken our innocent society. So, perhaps a good starting point for our analysis of living with the virus is to find the pandemic within ourselves.

Towards the end of Albert Camus' classic and, in the light of the current pandemic, eerily prescient novel *La Peste* about a plague epidemic in the Algerian city of Oran, one of the characters, Tarrou, makes a startling comment. 'To make things simpler, Rieux, let me begin by saying I had plague already, long before I came to this town and encountered it here' (Camus, 1948, 222). Although he has tirelessly organised volunteer groups to tend to the sick and dying, and will later die of the disease himself, at the time of his conversation with his friend Dr Rieux, Tarrou is not afflicted by the disease. His subsequent words make clear that he intends his statement to be understood metaphorically: 'Which is tantamount to saying I'm like everybody else. Only there are some people who don't know it, or feel at ease in that condition; others know and want to get out of it. Personally, I've always wanted to get out of it' (Camus, 1948, 222).

Tarrou then relates how a particular incident in his youth – witnessing his father, a judge, condemn a man to death – changed his life. He realises that he cannot accept a society that condones the death sentence, leaves home at the age of 17 and, over the course of several decades, joins a number of insurrectionary movements. When one day he witnesses the execution of a traitor to the cause, he realises that all this time he also has, unbeknownst to himself, passively excused the killing of fellow humans, this time in the name of justice and liberation. He cannot accept any killing that is sanctioned by authorities of whatever stripe and turns away in shame and disgust, fruitlessly looking for inner peace:

> For many years I've been ashamed, mortally ashamed, of having been, even with the best intentions, even at many removes, a murderer in my turn. As time went on I merely learned that even those who were better than the rest could not keep themselves nowadays from killing or letting others kill, because such is the logic by which they live; and that we can't stir a finger in this world without the risk of bringing death to somebody. (Camus, 1948, 228)

Tarrou's monologue is one of the highlights of a novel that itself is intended to be read as an extended simile of cruel, indifferent fate and the range of human attempts to come to terms with that. Tarrou's story seems to resonate with the current COVID-19 pandemic. But as with all parables, its meaning, although vivid, is not obvious. Tarrou seems to imply that somehow, we are all implicated in the pandemic. That statement can be interpreted in at least three different ways, some more helpful than others for understanding our predicament and charting an adequate response to it.

The most obvious interpretation is that wittingly and unwittingly each and every one of us – at least in the rich world – has contributed to the pandemic's occurrence. That makes us guilty of multiple bad habits such as overconsumption, excessive and frivolous travel, buying inexpensive flash fashion, indulging in a meat-rich diet, driving an SUV, and so on. Each of these habits has not only contributed to catastrophic climate change but has also been responsible for sustaining large inequalities in wealth, social position, gender and race – within societies, but also on a global scale, between the northern and southern hemisphere. Our consumption habits have, among other things, contributed to rainforest and habitat destruction, and possibly even to the incursion of the virus in the human habitat. By disrupting these ecosystems and catching and killing the animals that inhabit it, we have been 'shaking the viruses loose from their hosts' (Quammen, 2020; Pálsson, 2020, 11). Quammen shows that the SARS-CoV-2 virus is only the latest in a grim list of deadly viruses that have made the jump from animals to humans. So, in a straightforward and direct sense, we all have been carrying the pandemic within ourselves all the time. To fight it we need to urgently change our destructive habits.

Although there is an almost obvious truth to this explanation of our current predicament, and will no doubt satisfy our sense of moral indignation, it is also misleading. We can take our cue from another feature of Tarrou's parable: its pervasive humanism. Tarrou says that, with few exceptions, people do not have a cruel desire for the death penalty; we justify it as a necessary evil with seemingly compelling arguments. Everyone carries the death penalty, the plague, within themselves (Camus, 1948, 229). Tarrou seems to say that the plague, although not willed by us, is the inevitable by-product of our way of life, of the collective practices and arrangements which define our lifestyle. In a remarkable paper the British social scientist Elisabeth Shove (2010) comments on the futility of the so-called ABC model of social change – Attitude, Behaviour, Choice – in climate matters. The ABC model situates the responsibility for change within the individual and perhaps for this reason it has been popular with policy makers. It stipulates that climate change can be addressed if individuals can be convinced to change their 'behaviour' – while it 'obscures the extent to which governments sustain unsustainable economic institutions and ways of life, and the extent to which they have a hand in structuring options and possibilities' (Shove, 2010, 1274).

Such focus on individual behaviour is of course part of a larger trend to place the onus for changing problematic phenomena on individual people. A case in point is the current trend of behavioural interventions in public policy, epitomised by the hype around 'nudging' (Prainsack, 2020a). Policy makers see the tackling of the 'demand side' of policy problems, instead of changing the 'supply side', as a particularly innovative idea. Let's 'nudge' people to eat less and exercise more to fight the obesity 'epidemic'. The implication is that, if people can be convinced to make the right 'choices' (a term deeply couched in consumer culture), then it will not be necessary to improve the social and economic determinants that shape obesity. Think of the lack of time to exercise, the lack of parks and safe pavements for walking, the pull of nonstop advertising inveigling us to consume processed food, and the stress and existential worry that makes eating, drinking, smoking and binge-watching a coping strategy. The American economists Anne Case and Angus Deaton (2020) famously coined the term 'deaths of despair' to refer to the phenomenon that more and more people in the rich world no longer have any motivation to stay healthy and fit, or even alive; there is nothing for them to live for. (How health status related to poverty and stigma is involved in shaping COVID risk will be discussed in Chapter 3.)

Shove (2010) presents a different approach to social change in the context of the climate catastrophe, an approach that is also applicable to other problems. She argues that people act in ways that are detrimental to the climate not necessarily because of carelessness or indifference but because they are carriers of practices. Practices are configurations of beliefs, action and material artefacts that make up and structure our everyday world. We will return to the important concept of practice in the next chapter. Here we just conclude that social practices shape our behaviour and they give meaning to the world around us. They are the building blocks of performance and in the process make the world as we know it appear natural and self-evident. We do not buy a car, fly across the continent for a weekend trip, shove convenience food in the microwave because we do not care about our health or the natural environment. We do so because our social environment is structured in such a way that our choices in these matters are prearranged. There might be no public transport to bring us to our workplace. The working day might be too long to cook a meal from fresh ingredients. And a barrage of travel advertising plus a global mass tourism industry makes it possible to think that flying hundreds of miles to spend our weekend is a good idea (and, given the heavily subsidised low prices of budget air travel, perhaps cheaper than spending a weekend in bars and restaurants in our own country). The structure of practices that make up our everyday world programmes us to engage in destructive behaviour. Practices present us with a morally ambiguous situation, however. While they structure our world, by engaging in a practice we also sustain it. The pandemic is within us through our practices.

There is a third interpretation of Tarrou's parable, one that complicates the involvement of the individual human agent in the pandemic even more. It has become commonplace to designate our age as the Anthropocene (Pálsson, 2020, 17). The term has different meanings. In a strict geological sense, as a successor to earlier geologic eras such as the Jurassic, Pleistocene or Holocene, it has been contested. Enduring remnants of human influence on the Earth's deep structure are rare although species extinction and so-called plastiglomerates (agglomerates of naturally occurring materials and hardened molten plastic) are undeniable signs of the fusion of the geological and the social (Pálsson, 2020, 79). In its wider meaning, of the destructive impact of human life on the planet, the Anthropocene has become a household term. It draws our attention to the range of 'actors' – animals, plants, microorganisms, glaciers, oceans, wetlands, viruses, fungi, humans – and the complex, intersecting flows between them that shape the health of our planet and that are negatively impacted by human activity.

Bronislaw Szerszynski (2019) has argued that the social sciences need a 'planetary turn'. With this he draws attention to the many interlocking features of our planet – gases, molecules, atoms, subatomic particles, flows of energy, microorganisms, and so on, operating on different scales of time and space – that determine its past and present state. But above all he shows how these invisible features of the planet 'make possible and also condition human life' (Szerszynski, 2019, 225). Since the first industrial revolution the organisation of economic and political life has been predicated on the presumption that nature is external to the social. Nature is something to be conquered and exploited for the benefit of humans. The notion of the Anthropocene has confronted us with the sharp realisation that natural and social history are continuous (Pálsson, 2020, 10). Humans are as much in the planet as the planet is in us.

The problem with the concept of the Anthropocene is that, similar to the notion of practice, there is a certain disconnect between its aggregate import and individual, willed behaviour. While it is obvious that frequent flying, driving a diesel-propelled car or eating a meat-rich diet has deleterious effects on the natural environment (and many of these practices are bad for our health as well), most effects are mediated through larger institutional structures; structures that are subject to the law of large numbers. Eating meat compels us to participate in a global food production chain that includes the destruction of the rainforest to make way for soybean production. The prevalence of hormones in our food with the attendant risk of inducing antimicrobial resistance in humans and the presence of slaughterhouses and meat packing facilities that exploit human labour are Petri-dishes for SARS-CoV-2 infections (Pollan, 2020). We will see in the next chapter that the influence of human agency on the planet is mediated through the laws of complexity. That does not absolve us from our moral duty to work towards a sustainable and humane society, but it makes the diagnosis of what is wrong with our current political-economic order, and why it turns out to be so difficult to change it for the better, much more difficult.

We draw two important conclusions from this analysis of human agency and the dysfunctional political-economic order that has been exposed by the COVID-19 crisis. The first is that change is not merely a matter of inducing people to alter their behaviour. Social practices and the continuity between the human and the planetary order suggest that both the problem and its possible solutions must be sought at a higher level of aggregation. Solutions can only be collective solutions. That moves the analysis into the realm of public policy and democratic decision making.

Second, the deep entanglement of the natural and the social precludes a quick fix to the COVID-19 crisis. Vaccination programmes and drugs will play an important role in avoiding infections and treating the symptoms of COVID-19, but there will be no post-COVID era, no new normal. New viruses will jump across the animal human divide. Other species – such as fungi – might threaten our health and livelihood. High-tech fixes, with their tendency to individualise both the problem and the 'cure', will not solve these problems. We need to find ways to live more in harmony with our social needs and natural environment. This small book will suggest a comprehensive and interconnected series of collective measures to do just that. But first we need to further articulate our diagnosis of what the problem is in the first place.

2

At home in the world: overcoming the predicament of complexity and hegemony

The human predicament

The last 40 to 50 years have witnessed extraordinary economic growth and technological development. While in many countries, particularly, but not exclusively, in the developed world, large numbers of people have experienced unprecedented prosperity and security from an array of social risks, the way we have organised our society and economy has eaten away at the very foundations that made this growth possible. These foundations are environmental, social and moral. Thousands of books, blogs and op-eds have been written to diagnose the destructive processes that have resulted in environmental degradation, unprecedented inequalities in wealth and income, the hollowing out of labour contracts and worker representation and the associated decline in wages, social misery for millions through unnecessarily tight fiscal policies, structural racism and sexism, and the erosion of democracy in many countries. It should not have taken COVID-19 for us to realise that things have to change, and that the way we organise our economy is killing people and the planet.

There are different ways to describe the problems revealed by the COVID-19 crisis – mess, wreckage, plight, policy catastrophe – each with its own distinct moral tinge and call for transformation. For reasons we explain in this chapter we have decided to settle for 'predicament'. Trying to stave off the theological overtones that the term might generate, the social theorist William Connolly (2011) calls a predicament an 'existential condition'. What does this mean? First, that it concerns a state or condition that we cannot walk away from and that it is, at least partly, out of our hands. It cannot be mastered (we will return to the notion of mastery in Chapter 5). This depiction tends towards the tragic – not a sentiment that we gladly evoke in our instrumental age – and not surprisingly Connolly refers to Sophocles to get his point across: 'Our predicament involves how to negotiate life, without hubris or existential resentment, in an age that is neither providential nor susceptible to consummate mastery. We must explore how to invest existential affirmation in such a world, even if we strive to fend off its worst dangers.' (Connolly, 2011, 98) Predicament is not fatalism, however. It redirects the focus towards the lived experience and the urge to improve things. Not redemption but an optimistic belief in the powers of imagination and cooperation in the face of so much failure and anger; a desire for a better way of being. Awareness of predicament as a human condition engenders utopian thinking.

The utopian impulse is elemental to human experience, and possibly an anthropological given. It is a deep-seated desire for betterment, for overcoming the inevitable shortcomings of our current situation. Utopia, as the British sociologist Ruth Levitas says, is informed, educated hope (2013, 5). There is a strain of sceptical thought that equates utopia with an ill-advised, unrealistic striving for purity and perfection that easily descends into totalitarianism. Humans and their institutions are imperfect and inconsistent; history has demonstrated again and again that to try to impose utopian perfectibility onto flawed human nature will only result in violence and oppression (Gray, 2007). This anti-utopianism conflates utopia with perfection, state power and wholesale ideological blueprints. While history is littered with such ill-fated projects, it is misguided to characterise these as utopian. (Millenarian, namely the belief in the coming radical, ruthless overhaul of the social order, would be a better term.) The utopian impulse originates in human imperfection and never strays far from it. Although it strives to overcome the limitations of our current situation, it does not confuse emergent possibility with impossibility (Levitas, 2013, 17). Utopia is not about denying real human needs or projecting unlimited satisfactions. Levitas quotes the utopia scholar J.C. Davies who describes the defining characteristic of utopia as: 'the proposal of institutional means for managing the inevitable gap between want and satisfaction and the potential social conflicts that flow from this discrepancy' (Levitas, 2013, 10). Utopian thinking in this sense has both a critical and creative function. It makes the familiar unfamiliar, it disrupts what is taken for granted (Levitas, 2013, 4) and it 'facilitates holistic thinking about possible futures' (Levitas, 2013, xi). By imagining the possibility of human flourishing in a situation that is far from perfect, utopian thinking provides hope and consolation. At least we can imagine a world that is otherwise, and ward off alienation by reconnecting with self and others. We will return to the different functions of utopian thinking later in this chapter, as we believe that genuine utopian thinking (not the search of 'realistic' utopias that is so *en vogue* these days) can help us get unstuck from the reality that got us in trouble. But first we need to clarify what we mean by the human predicament in collective action.

The reason for our poor record in solving society's current ills can be summarised with two words: *complexity* and *hegemony*. Both of these terms signify large, inconclusive practical and intellectual challenges that afflict every policy initiative, no matter the societal domain or political regime. The best we can do here is to introduce the issues and sketch some of the implications of taking complexity and hegemony seriously in understanding the problems that beset us. But let us first emphasise the road we have *not* taken. We do not marshal the usual argument that the organised resistance of political and economic elites to progressive politics is to blame – a progressive politics that aspires to equal opportunity, sustainability and the wellbeing of the many.

We do not, of course, deny the existence of widespread corporate lobbying, the deliberate misinformation spread by the billionaire press, the erosion of good government, and the greed of an underhanded financial sector. We will discuss all these developments and some possible solutions, in the chapters to come. But laying our current predicament at the feet of the political and corporate elite, although morally satisfying, is not particularly helpful. It suggests that the solution is relatively easy: kick the bastards out and bring in a progressive, reform-minded group of rulers. We are probably not the only ones who are sceptical of this solution. Instead, ours is a plea for a system change in the spirit of humility and openness and the continuously proliferating possibilities of what Connolly (2011) calls a world of becoming. Whatever solutions are available to our current predicament, they will have to be collective and they will have to speak to the needs and aspirations of human communities, and the constraints and affordabilities of our natural environment. That means that there are no easy solutions and quick fixes. But an attitude of humility also opens up a wide space of human ingenuity, ethical awareness and spiritual fulfilment.

Complexity and the defeat of optimism

Complexity wreaks havoc with good intentions. In the words of the complexity scholar John Sterman, policy resistance, 'the tendency for interventions to be defeated by the response of the system to the intervention itself' (2002, 2), is endemic in public policy. He provides a dispiriting list of policies that, on the face of it perfectly reasonable, worsened the very condition they set out to improve. Policy resistance is the result of the denial of complexity. For, while we understand the separate parts of the problem, we have a hard time grasping how they are connected. The human brain is not hardwired to grasp complexity and the brain of the politician even less. Sterman (2002, 5) puts it as follows: 'Policy resistance arises from the mismatch between the dynamic complexity of the systems we have created and our cognitive capacity to understand that complexity.' So, what is complexity and how can we deal with it productively?

To talk of complex systems is to talk of the deep structure of the world that we inhabit. Complexity cannot be wished away. In that sense it is not merely a theory (although we make theoretical statements about the morphology of complex systems and their dynamic development). Instead it is a feature of (material) reality, like solidity, temperature or light. It is a feature not of individual actors (the 'elements') but of the system as a whole, emerging from the interaction between its parts: such as liquidity, which is not attributable to the individual H_2O atoms but emerges as joint property of interacting atoms. Neither is it a choice, as the Dutch complexity scholar Lasse Gerrits (2012, 18) states: 'It just *is* – it is self-generating.' It is this unsettled, unpredictable, permanently evolving character of complexity that trips up policy makers, and everyone else who aspires to benign intervention.

Complexity scholars attribute the dynamic quality of complex systems to a number of characteristics. *Dynamic complexity* arises from the interactions between the elements of a system, not so much the features of the elements themselves. An internal combustion engine has many parts but is not complex because each of its elements interacts in a tightly engineered way with only a few other parts. That is why the engine operates in a predictable way. A family has only a few members (let us say, two parents and three children) but is nevertheless a small complex system as each member interacts intensively and, as every parent can testify, often unpredictably, with each of the other members. These interactions result in unforeseen, or in the jargon of complexity theory, *emergent outcomes*. Thus, the state of a complex system is always emergent. Much used examples are the fluidity of water (the aforementioned example of the interaction of H_2O molecules) and consciousness (individual brain neurons do not possess consciousness, this is the result of the interaction of millions of them; Wagenaar, 2007). Emergence means that the whole cannot be explained by the characteristics of its parts. This flies in the face of conventional policy making where we tend to use the features of the individual elements as our leverage points for collective intervention. Thus, we attribute people's obesity or climate-destructive habits to their wasteful or profligate habits and try to persuade or nudge them to change these, instead of developing a more holistic understanding of the structural causes of these behaviours.

The interactions in a complex system are governed by *feedback*. Sterman (2002, 6), talking about human systems, puts this as follows: 'Our decisions alter the state of the world, causing changes in nature and triggering others to act, thus giving rise to a new situation which then influences our next decisions.' Feedback can be *positive*, increasing certain effects, for example when the warming of the Earth's atmosphere through a rise in CO_2 levels melts the permafrost that releases methane gas, that melts glaciers and arctic ice, reducing the expanse of bright, sun-reflecting surface, contributing even more to global warming, and so on. Feedback can also be *negative*, curtailing these effects, as when a product, think of the fax machine, is overtaken by more convenient technology such as emails and scans, gradually making it obsolete.

Feedback has two consequences that are essential to understanding complexity and that impede collective intervention: nonlinearity and co-evolution. Nonlinearity means that the effect in a system is not proportional to its cause and that proximate causes have distant effects. For example, awarding a mortgage to a family in the state of Nevada who cannot afford it (a so-called subprime mortgage) will result in financial hardship for that particular family. When a large number of subprime mortgages are packaged with high quality mortgages, commodified as derivatives, and sold on to banks and pension funds, they might result in the breakdown of the financial system, as the events of 2008 showed. The challenge of nonlinearity is that policy makers are often attracted to the proximate effect instead of the distant cause. There are sometimes good reasons for this. The immediate symptom can be so threatening or unacceptable (high SARS-CoV-2 virus infection rates) that authorities have a moral duty to act on it. However, symptom management often results in dismal cycles of ineffective or only partly effective policy responses (a vaccine that reaches only a part of the population, instead of dealing with the underlying cause of loss of biodiversity or alleviating poverty). As the policy scholar Aaron Wildavksy (1979, 62) put it a generation ago: policy is its own cause.

Co-evolution is an even more difficult aspect of complexity as it merges with hegemony, to be discussed below. *Co-evolution* means that each agent finds itself in an environment produced by its interactions with the other agents in the system. Actors are thus constantly acting and reacting to a changed and changing environment (Wagenaar, 2007, 9). More importantly, the principle of co-evolution implies that we are never outside a complex system. Again, this flies in the face of conventional policy making habits in which officials manage societal sectors from an external vantage point. But this is a fatal illusion, as we are always part and parcel of the very system we try to change. For example, since the financial crisis of 2008 central banks have turned to so-called quantitative easing to increase the amount of money in the financial system. Through a combination of ultra-low interest rates and making money available to banks, the expectation was that the latter would lend this money to businesses and thus stimulate the economy. However, banks did not increase the volume of loans. Instead, they used the money to bolster their capital requirements, as stipulated by government regulation. Those who held capital and were looking for decent returns in a low interest rate environment created real estate and stock market bubbles. And large transnational corporations took advantage of the situation to take on new debt, not to invest, but to engage in share buy-backs. (Share buy-backs are a method by which a publicly listed company buys its own shares on the stock market, thus reducing the number of outstanding shares. This increases the share price, the remuneration of top managers, and decreases the firm's resiliency to economic downturns.) 'Yesterday's solutions are today's problems', as Sterman (2002, 8) caustically summarises it.

Can we escape the unpredictability and uncontrollability of dynamic complexity in public policy making? Can we constrain this giant? Sterman admonishes us to think holistically. We should design mental models of the systemic nature of the problem at hand, a 'feedback view of the world'. That is sound but limited advice. One of the fundamental problems of dynamic complexity is that the 'system' is inherently unbounded. Everything is related to everything else, so the point where you decide to draw a boundary around the system is more or less arbitrary, decided by your policy goals or your ideology. Sterman provides an extended example where he shows how General Motors' failure to include its leasing operation into its analysis of new car sales led it to operate two business lines that worked against each other. Yet, he does not acknowledge that improved car sales and leasing increases the use of oil and global warming. This is not oversight on his part; it is simply outside the remit of his consignment, an all too common feature in the world of bureaucratic specialisation. Thinking holistically by modelling a complex system is obviously an important strategy. But perhaps, given the immense space of possibilities that a complex system presents, it is too daunting a task.

Given the fundamental unpredictability of complex dynamic systems, two policy scholars, Robert Axelrod and Michael Cohen, asked themselves how we can harness complexity, rather than try to reduce it, or act as if it is not there. How can we transform the overwhelming confluence of flows into a positive force? 'Seeking to improve ... without being able fully to control' as they phrase it (2000, xvi). They suggest three simple but powerful strategies: encourage variety, change interaction patterns and build on successful outcomes. By encouraging variety, the system increases its chances that it is adapted to future changes in its external environment. By changing interaction patterns, actors meet other actors (including natural, material agents) with different experiences, knowledge and perspectives, thereby expanding the repertoire of solutions, at the same time building social networks of trust, understanding and cooperative engagement. Selection means the growth and spread of valued criteria to foster evolutionary learning in the system (Axelrod and Cohen, 2000, 155–158). These three strategies add up to an open, inclusive, and collaborative policy environment. We will return to this conclusion in Chapter 10 where we discuss the democratic implications of our analysis.

Hegemony as cognitive captivity

One of the themes throughout this book is the awareness that in public policy so often good intentions end up awry and good advice falls on deaf ears. One important reason is the surreptitious power of hegemony. Hegemony is one of those terms that in academic circles has led to the kind of endless, exasperating expositions that are usually reserved for the politics of the Vatican. One common meaning of hegemony is a lasting grip on power that allows the power holder to dominate a political arena effectively and enduringly. In a world where dog eats dog, hegemony in this sense is something to strive for, and the thinker who is forever associated with this meaning of the term is Machiavelli. A second meaning of hegemony is ideological dominance, famously associated with the Italian Marxist thinker Antonio Gramsci. It has a number of advantages over the Machiavellian concept of hegemony in that it recognises that hegemonic dominance is as much cultural as political, that its effectiveness depends on its ability to conceal its *modus operandi* to the point that it appears the taken-for-granted natural state of affairs, and that it requires the implicit concurrence of the public.

Our concept of hegemony extends the latter aspect of hegemony, as a form of unrecognised cognitive captivity. Hegemony is a situation in which we are unable to see beyond our cognitive, moral and practical horizon. We live, work, breathe and appreciate in a world that makes sense to us. Where most of the time situations are reassuringly self-evident because we have been socialised into a system of judgements, of ways of seeing and doing. The shape of that world, its obvious, uncontested meaning, is hardwired into our very language. It is a cultural, experiential default position as it were. When, for example, we hear every expert, politician and news anchor use the word 'economy' over and over again, we assume that that there is an entity, separate from the rest of society and in opposition to the natural environment, that is administered by experts (business managers, economists, the financial press, central banks and so on), operating according to its own rules, that is somehow vital to everyone's wellbeing, and the smooth functioning of which overrides every other concern. That imagery is confirmed day in, day out by the reporting of indicators such as changes in Gross Domestic Product, the number of unemployed, the rate of inflation, and so on. We assume the existence of the economy, and even when we are critical of certain aspects of it (such as large inequalities in wealth, or its contribution to global warming), it does not occur to us to question the category itself.

The incontestable character of our everyday reality is dependent on the essentially bounded nature of our habits, perceptions and even sensibilities. Wittgenstein, the thinker associated with this meaning of hegemony, gave a famous illustration. Think of someone, he said, who is imprisoned in a room with the door unlocked. How can that be? He has been socialised all his life with doors opening outwards, while this one opens inwards. It simply does not occur to him to pull at the door instead of pushing it in vain (Owen, 2003, 85). That is hegemony. Pushing the door of our neoliberal world order instead of pulling it and walking inside another, better world.

In the pages that follow we will repeatedly return to the neoliberal nature of our political economy. The term neoliberal has been used as an epithet so often that it has practically lost its meaning. What we mean by the term is a worldview that proclaims the efficiency of unregulated, self-correcting markets and the intrinsic ineffectiveness of a discredited state (Kuttner, 2018, xvii). Although as an ideology it had been around for the larger part of the 20th century, its stunning global ascent throughout the world started in earnest at the beginning of the 1970s. We will tell some of that story in Chapter 6 when we describe its implications for government, and we will return to it in the chapters in which we discuss corporate responsibility and the reform of the finance system. What is important here is to accentuate the extent to which the precepts of neoliberalism have not only taken over their 'natural' domains of business and finance, but also government and even private lives. The colonisation of our personal desires, aspirations and sentiments by a doctrine of individualism, personal responsibility and continuous self-improvement has at least one commentator speak of 'everyday neoliberalism' (Mirowski, 2014). The doctrine of neoliberalism has closed off our horizon and restricted our ability to imagine an alternative social order. That is hegemony, and although rooted in ideology, it goes beyond it.

The British political theorist David Owen has pointed out that what makes it difficult not only to break free from hegemony as cognitive capacity but even to recognise it as such, is that it is not about something being true or false. Hegemony is not a matter of holding false beliefs or a system of beliefs such as an ideology. This is an important realisation as it is relevant to the possibility of the kind of positive social change that we propose in this book. Someone can be held captive by a belief (for example that SARS-CoV-2 was developed in a laboratory in China and deliberately released to undermine the western world) or an ideology (for example that socialism inevitably results in tyranny). In both of these cases it is in principle possible to point out the erroneousness of the belief or ideology, although we might not be able to sway the person holding them. Hegemony, instead, concerns the very intelligibility of our world, the way we determine what can be judged true or false in the first place. The 'economy', as we discussed it in the preceding paragraph, as a separate realm, performing to its own laws, to be managed by people with specialised knowledge, is not true or false, it just *is*. This image of the economy is the tacit background of our lifeworld, somewhat like a landscape or cityscape. We live in it, but we don't see it.

Hegemony is not just cognitive, it also has a firm hold over our ethical appreciations. Hegemony imposes a particular moral order and a hierarchy of ascendency on society. It confers intellectual authority to designated experts and, conversely, withholds it from others, such as ordinary citizens or peripheral groups. Think of the awe with which the pronouncements of central bank presidents or captains of industry are received by the media. But hegemony also shapes moral sensibility. It instructs us how to feel. We are willing to take a bet that 50 years from now we will experience a historical shock when we read how governments demonised welfare recipients, condemned hundreds of thousands to a precarious existence by abolishing worker protections and fighting unions, or destroyed precious public sector institutions by handing them over to private corporations. Or that we condoned an economic system that forced retirees out of their homes and into a precarious nomadic life. Or that immensely wealthy and powerful transnational corporations got away with wholesale tax avoidance. Or that we put a public good, money, into the hands of private actors, banks, and repeatedly spent hundreds of billions of taxpayers' money to bail them out when they speculated it away. We imagine how historians will quote how tweets suggesting rights for workers or state-regulated universal health are met with angry cries of 'socialism' or 'show us where this has ever worked'. We are not painting a fantasy where all these things are not happening anymore but a world where the moral inertia towards these destructive aspects of our economic and political order will be met with astonishment. That is hegemony at work for you here.

This combination of cognitive and moral captivity makes it so very difficult to grasp the essentially arbitrary nature of these hegemonic images. They constrain our perception, our sensibility, and our repertoire of activities to the point that we cannot even imagine that things could be different. Moreover, what makes a hegemonic situation truly hermetic is its interconnectedness. As we saw in the preceding chapter, the world is self-evident because it rests on a bundle of practices, into which we have been thoroughly socialised and which are held in place by institutions, beliefs, understandings, ideologies and identities. This is where hegemony and complexity meet. Try to reform one aspect of this dense structure (for example, introduce sustainable production methods) and you run into another set of institutions and practices that pushes back (the international finance system, or the large network of carbon subsidies, for example). Resistance to change is not so much a psychological quality, as Elisabeth Shove (2010) pointed out, but the effect of being caught in a web of practices. When the solutions to improve a given situation are framed in the same terms as the very situation you seek to change, you know you are in a hegemonic situation. Or, reversely, when some reasonable proposals are met with incredulity, dismissed as impractical or not worthy of serious discussion, this is another sure sign that you find yourself caught up in a hegemonic situation.

The utopian method of social transformation

Taken together complexity and hegemonic captivity are our human predicament. An existential condition that is indifferent to our preferences and aspirations. If you are a climate activist or climate change denier, a hard-nosed neoliberal or a committed socialist, you cannot avoid the laws of complexity and the surreptitious influence of hegemonic captivity. They raise their heads as soon as you leave the realm of discourse to put your ideals into practice. How do we ever liberate ourselves from this predicament? The answer is that we should be attentive to our utopian impulse. As we saw earlier, to engage in utopian thinking is an affirmation of our essential humanity, an exploration of the manifold possibilities of life.

In the course of writing this book we found ourselves – admittedly somewhat to our surprise – engaging with a wide and long western tradition of utopian writing. Or perhaps it is better to speak of a deep-seated human need to imagine a better, more inspiring alternative to a burdening, oppressive present. Some commentators go as far as to see utopian thinking, 'the urge to transcend', as a 'universal feature of the human condition' (Bauman, 1976, in Levitas, 2013, 106). Throughout history thinkers, theologians, and philosophers have drawn imaginary worlds of harmony and of longing for a commonwealth of equality, dignity, an understanding God's works, and, nowadays, a reciprocal relationship with our natural environment (Manuel and Manuel, 1979, 211; Purdy, 2019).

Ruth Levitas has done us the immense service of rendering the utopian impulse into a systematic, generative, open-ended method. While some critics paint a caricaturist picture of utopian thinking as an impractical, escapist activity with little or no practical relevance to our flawed everyday reality, Levitas has shown how utopian thinking was formative in the institutionalisation of sociology as a scientific discipline at the turn of the 20th century. And although hard science prevailed eventually, the impulse to imagine, holistically, narratively, future-oriented, a better society as the basis for normative social critique has always been a lively undercurrent in sociology.

According to Levitas, utopian thinking fulfils three important functions in social thought: compensation, critique and change (Levitas, 2013, 107). As such, it is a *method* – a systematic and integrative approach to transcend our hegemonic present and to harness its intrinsic interconnectedness. Levitas has provided us with the critical and conceptual tools of the utopian method. They help us to analyse the limitations of our policy endeavours and suggest possible futures. Perhaps even more importantly, the utopian method restores moral imagination to its rightful place in public and academic discourse. After surveying the various risks and pitfalls of utopian thought (noncommittal, transcendental fantasy, the unthinking projection of our current imperfect institutions into the future, an exclusive emphasis on the critical function of utopia, a propensity to see utopias as closed blueprints instead of a provisional and reflexive dialogue), Levitas presents a tripartite approach to utopian thinking. It consists of three elements or 'modes', as she calls them. An 'archaeological' mode in which we construct or reconstruct a particular image of the good society. An 'ontological' mode in which we address the question of what kind of people specific social and institutional arrangements encourage. 'What is understood as human flourishing, what capabilities are valued, encouraged, and genuinely enabled, or blocked and suppressed, by specific existing or potential social arrangements: we are concerned here with the historical and social determination of human nature.' (Levitas, 2013, 153) And an 'architectural' mode which is concerned with the design of alternative institutional and social arrangements that bring about the desired form of human flourishing.

Together, these three modes add up to a coherent and responsible strategy of 'informed, educated hope' (Levitas, 2013, 5). In this little book we will mostly concern ourselves with institutional design, the architectural mode of utopia, with occasional excursions to the historical and capability elements, the important questions of how we got here and who we want to be. This is not because we think that this expansion of our imagination is less important but simply because of the nature of our project. We are both trained as policy scholars. This book is an attempt to restore moral vision to policy analysis, this most practical and mundane of academic disciplines. It is a small manifesto of better, more imaginative, more hopeful, policy making.

It is all well and good to promote utopia as a method for genuine social change, but we are under no illusion about the difficulties of changing entrenched institutions. The challenge is not only to look beyond our cognitive horizons – after all, the human capacity for creative imagination is almost boundless – but also to overcome our emotional restrictions. The first, necessary, step in utopia as method is to transform our criticism of a particular state of affairs into a genuine estrangement or alienation with that particular situation. We need to invest our awareness that something is not right, with emotion and authenticity. As a result, the problem goes from being abstract to embodied and in that way, we transform a rather noncommittal cognitive understanding into an urgent sense of estrangement.

That is a difficult step to take as such estrangement carries identity costs for the individual. While it is relatively easy to agree, in reading a newspaper article or in a discussion with a friend, about what is wrong with society (for example, the mistreatment of animals in the global food production chain, or the CO_2 emissions caused by the production of beef), it is much more difficult to walk away from authentic estrangement. Most of us can live quite well with considerable levels of cognitive dissonance and continue with our habitual ways of doing things (for example, unthinkingly ordering a steak in a restaurant). The emotional costs of alienation, however, make us feel acutely uncomfortable about the situation at hand, and about ourselves for condoning it. They urge us to do something about it. Experiencing estrangement means that we move from an abstract, superficial understanding of the damaging situation to grasping it in the round. This is because the many implications that the adverse situation, and its improvement, has for the organisation of our institutions and our private lives unspools before our eyes. We are able and willing to stare the situation in the face, unflinching. Taken together this adds up to a sense of urgency to do something about it. This is the passion of, for example, Greta Thunberg, that drives her to travel the globe to confront political leaders with the gap between their rhetoric and their actions on climate change and endure nasty personal attacks by her opponents. Utopian estrangement both requires and engenders moral courage.

Once the taken-for-granted nature of the present has become unfamiliar, the positive work of utopias as architecture begins. We can begin with imagining and designing alternative institutional arrangements that bring about the desired form of human flourishing. Not by projecting an improved version of the current situation into the future but instead by articulating the society we desire and design the institutions and social relations that make it possible (Levitas, 2013, 198).

Utopia as method does not guarantee the overcoming of the predicament of being captive to our practices and understandings, and it certainly is no recipe for harnessing the laws of complexity when we venture out to try to realise our ideals. But it is the only way we have of overcoming our unrecognised alienation from ourselves, from our ideals and feelings, from our families, work and environment, and to engage in imagining, designing and realising a home in the world. This will be the task in the remainder of this book.

3

Ensuring a well-functioning public infrastructure

In this and the six following chapters we will present what we believe are the elements that are required for a better world for humans and for the planet. None of these solutions are new: each one of them has been proposed and tried out in one form or another before. But rarely have they been presented in connection with each other. For example, while politicians on the Left have long argued for an improvement of public infrastructure, they are more reluctant to present concrete ideas to tackle the dysfunctional global financial order. But the latter is a condition of possibility for the former. In the preceding chapter we argued that, next to hegemony, another reason that it is so difficult to get a grip on the pandemic and its fallout is its complexity – not in the trivial, but in the non-linear dynamics sense of the word. Complexity means that everything hangs together in a constantly evolving way. The development of complex systems is unpredictable not because people are too ignorant, unintelligent, or have too little evidence; it is unpredictable because the interaction of the elements in complex systems creates new, unforeseen outcomes. Complexity concerns policy because almost all spaces where humans and other living beings live and act maintain dynamic connections with other spaces. So far, however, policy tends to approach the problems within its purview in a reductionist manner. It typically pretends that we can, or should be able to, act upon complex systems as if they were mechanical devices – often with negative or even perverse consequences, as we saw in Chapter 2. If we want to make better policy, we need to frame problems and design solutions in ways that are commensurate with dynamic complexity.

Thus, what we will do is to present a series of proposals for change as an integrated whole. Each one of them is an element of a new, more just, more sustainable, social-political and economic order. Taken together they embody a utopian vision of human flourishing. This holistic vision of reform allows us to start pulling, instead of foolhardily pushing, the door of neoliberal hegemony. In this chapter we will start with one of the most striking insights from the COVID-19 crisis: the importance of a well-functioning public infrastructure.

The importance of strong public infrastructures

Although this aspect has not received a lot of explicit attention in mainstream news media and discussions, what quickly became apparent during the first months of the COVID-19 crisis is that countries with good public infrastructures have dealt with the crisis much better than those that did not – in virtually every respect. Their healthcare systems were more resilient; tenants were protected against eviction; laid-off workers could rely on a social safety net.

While biological risk factors to suffer a severe course of COVID-19 – age, male gender, and pre-existing conditions such as cardiovascular or respiratory problems, or diabetes – received extensive coverage throughout the first months of the pandemic, the discussion of social and economic risk factors has largely been restricted to expert fora in academic journals. While policy experts got worked up over whether or not centralised or decentralised governance models are more effective in beating the pandemic, or whether countries with authoritarian rule or more extensive digital surveillance are better equipped to prevent new infections, only few commentators drew attention to the social and economic factors that determine COVID-19 related risks. These are not only social and economic risks, such as the loss of jobs or income, but also the medical risks of suffering complications, or getting infected in the first place. People who, as 'essential' or 'key' workers, rely on overcrowded public transportation to go to work, and who live together with others in small flats or houses cannot keep the necessary physical distance from others to avoid infection. Comorbidities and social factors interact to increase the COVID-19 disease burden of those who are already disadvantaged. Those with lower levels of education, smaller flats, less income, and more precarious employment before the crisis have been affected more strongly by income and job losses, conflicts within the family, anxiety, and other effects. These, in turn, are likely to negatively affect their health and their economic opportunities in the future. Social and economic disadvantage shapes the *biological* risk of suffering from COVID-19. Here is negative feedback in the complex system of population health at work.

Against this backdrop it seems particularly frustrating that much of the political response focuses only on short-term emergency measures to alleviate the most acute harms of the crisis. This is at the cost of addressing two of the most important root causes of

COVID risk, namely poverty and deficient public infrastructures. Public infrastructure has not been a very sexy topic in recent decades. As we will also show in Chapter 6, ideologies such as New Public Management (NPM), austerity and public debt aversion have firmly implanted deep into our collective consciousness the conviction that the public sector is less flexible, less effective and, overall, less beneficial to society than the private sector. That, combined with the growing traction of the idea that individual citizens should be held responsible for their health, employability and wellbeing, has resulted in an ever greater retreat of collective responsibility for satisfying the fundamental needs of the people.

In countries where the decline of public services and infrastructure had been particularly stark, such as in the United States and the United Kingdom, progressive thinkers had already started to draw attention to the need to bring back collective responsibility for meeting people's basic needs before the outbreak of the COVID-19 pandemic. A prominent example is the universal basic services (UBS) movement initiated by a group of academics at the Institute for Global Prosperity at University College London (Coote and Percy, 2020). In the centre of the UBS movement stands the satisfaction of needs that all people have in common: these fundamental needs (rather than wants) are the basic requirements to survive, to participate in society, and to live with a modicum of security and dignity. Some of these needs – such as food or clothing – can be satisfied by things that people can buy. Others – such as healthcare, elder- and childcare, housing, transport, education and information – cannot, or are more difficult to satisfy by people themselves and should thus be provided publicly.

UBS thus have three characteristics. First, they are services, understood as collectively generated activities that serve the public interest. Second, the services provided are basic, meaning that they are 'essential and sufficient (rather than minimal) to enable people to meet their needs'. Third, they are universal in the sense that everyone is entitled to these services, independent of their ability to pay (Coote and Percy, 2020, 4). Rather than a call for a return to the 'good old age' of the centralised provision of services, proponents of UBS want to 'overhaul the traditional model of public services so that they are genuinely participative, controlled by the people who need and use them, and supported rather than always directly provided by the state' (Coote and Percy, 2020, 5). The most important role of the state is to provide the legal framework within which these services will be provided, and to prescribe and monitor standards – while the provision of the services itself should take place through cooperatives, citizen initiatives and private vendors. The British UBS initiative covers services in the context of shelter, food, health, education, transport, information, and the legal and democratic domain (see also universalbasicservices.org). In a typical OECD country, the provision of UBS is estimated to amount to around 4.3 per cent of GDP (Coote and Percy, 2020, 115).

UBS is a thoughtful and well thought out proposal that carries the imprint of its origins: the dysfunctional and besieged public sector of the UK and the concomitant distrust of the state. While the authors say they are inspired by others who are thinking along the same lines, they omit to mention the public bureaucracies in many continental European countries – working in a tradition that goes back at least a century and a half – that provide comprehensive public services to the population at large. These public services work to the satisfaction of the largest part of the population. In Austria, our country of residence, water and energy are delivered by public companies. In the early 1900s, Karl Lueger, the Christian-Social mayor of Vienna – who is otherwise critically remembered as a populist using antisemitism as a political tool (Wistrich, 1983) – created a public gas company to undercut the oligopoly of mostly foreign energy companies. He also built a 100-kilometre-long aqueduct that is still in use today, to supply water from the Styrian Alps to the city. To this day, the national railways are run by a company owned by the Republic of Austria. The trains are frequent and comfortable. Tickets are affordable and can be purchased anytime at the station or online at a fixed price; price levels do not change with demand or time of day. When there is a lot of demand for trains, the Railway Corporation puts out more carriages or increases the frequency of trains. Concessions are available for trains at certain hours, or for concession card holders, but the price will only ever be lower, and not higher, than the standard price.

Lueger also bought out and consolidated the private companies that exploited the patchwork of private tram lines in the city and created an integrated public transport network. Today, for €365 per year, the roughly two million residents of Vienna can purchase a travel pass that gives them access to all public transportation within the greater municipal area. For one Euro per day (or less, if one is a senior or student or otherwise qualifies for concessions), they can make use of a well-integrated network of high-frequency trams, buses, underground lines and rapid overground trains. The characteristic Jugendstil architecture of public buildings such as underground stations, bridges, post offices and administrative offices was the result of the city's desire to express civic pride and the shared wealth of public space. The long and the short of it is that the citizens of Vienna enjoy a wide range of accessible and high quality public services that are provided by the state.

We do not want to privilege one model of service provision over another; both have advantages and disadvantages. Infrastructure, no matter how it is managed, requires constant investment for maintenance and modernisation or risk gradual decline. To maximise returns to shareholders private companies often skimp on investing in infrastructure, as the sad fate of water provision in the UK demonstrates. But the fact that infrastructure is publicly owned is no guarantee for sufficient investment either; instructive examples are the German railways, Italian bridges or the National Health Service (NHS) in England. We only want to point out that, in contrast to reigning administrative doctrine, there are alternative arrangements of public service delivery that are effective and equitable. Moreover, in practice the continental, state-led model converges with the UBS model in that in some countries, such as the Netherlands, services are provided by a mix of state bureaucracies, professional agencies, private actors, citizen initiatives and non-governmental organisations. In both instances the role of the state is, in addition to direct provision, to secure the financing, regulating and coordinating of this assemblage of service providers. The world after COVID-19 must include a well-functioning, secure and accessible public infrastructure, no matter how it is organised. Public infrastructure includes quality, accessible health care, ample social housing supported by tenant protection and rent control, good, affordable public transport, nationwide broadband and mobile phone coverage, affordable education at all levels, a social security system that mitigates the risks of life, and affordable legal services that allow every citizen the opportunity to challenge arbitrary or wrongful behaviour from government or business organisations. This is not just a matter of efficiency (increasing output and outcome while reducing the transaction costs of the service system) but also of the kind of society we envision (see Table 3.1).

One of the strengths of the proposal by authors Anna Coote and Andrew Percy is its broad view of the benefits of UBS. They do not only conceive of UBS in terms of efficiency (getting a bang for your buck), but also of equality, solidarity and sustainability. Yet, the emphasis on the functional requirement of efficiency comes at the cost of the more important point about the moral significance of a public infrastructure: its practical articulation of a vision of the good society and human capacities in relation to the institutions that bring them about – both the institutions we have and could have. UBS runs the risk this way of becoming yet another reform movement thereby

Table 3.1: What fundamental needs should be satisfied via universal basic services?

Service	What do we need?	How do we pay for it?
Education	Education up to college/university should be provided free at the point of use; higher education should be affordable to everyone without the requirement to take on excessive debt (by concessions on tuition fees for those from low-income families, and/or affordable loans provided by public banks or bodies)	↑
Healthcare	Should be provided free at the point of use, and free from formal and informal (educational, employment-related) barriers	Higher taxes on wealth; within the healthcare system, cost savings should be achieved through reducing waste (e.g. low-value interventions, overdiagnosis, and overtreatment; focusing on end-of-life care that offers social and palliative care as alternatives to invasive treatments)
Housing	Every resident should have access to stable housing of a certain size and quality at a set, low rent via unbreakable long-term leases. Risks of free riding should be reduced through laws that discourage ownership of more than one home per family, anti-speculation taxation, and heavy fines for fraudulent claims to subsidised public housing (for more details, see Chapter 4)	
Information	Public provision of Wi-Fi infrastructure, also in rural regions, and excellent mobile coverage at very low or no cost	
Transportation	Free local transportation for every resident; low-cost transportation options nationally. Public oversight, or public ownership, of the hardware and software of public transportation that needs to be frequent, reliable, in addition to being affordable	↓

Source: Authors, inspired by universalbasicservices.org

missing an opportunity for a more fundamental rethinking of the deeper question of human flourishing and how to bring it about.

They also run the risk of missing the moment. Social and political transformation is a long, hard toil with regular setbacks and uncertain payoffs. But every now and then, history slips into a vortex of wrenching crises where solutions and alternatives that used to be unthinkable suddenly move into the realm of the possible. Wars and major economic recessions have created such moments. We hope, and we believe, that the ongoing COVID-19 crisis is such a window for transformative change. We believe we can get there, but for that we need a vision to guide us and keep us on track when we are immersed in the toil of designing and implementing better policies. We need to engage in 'holistic thinking about possible futures', in, what, in the preceding chapter, we called 'utopia as method', the systematic imagining of alternatives to the current order. Such a vision is not the icing on the cake of practical reform. The articulation of a compelling story is, instead, the beating heart, the condition of possibility of successful social reform. As this insight is also relevant to the chapters to come, we will briefly explain our theory of institutional change.

The pragmatic relevance of utopian thinking

The link between Levitas' visionary utopianism and the practical work of institutional reform is contained in the philosophy of the 20th century American pragmatist philosopher John Dewey.[1] Dewey, in his lifetime a recognised public intellectual, social reformer and champion of democracy, inspired generations of scholars in public policy and organisational studies. He famously formulated an approach to social reform that rested on three 'pillars': a consistent focus on concrete problems, reflexivity and deliberation. (Although Dewey was a philosopher, similar to Follett (see note 1), he had little patience with his profession's penchant for abstract theorising.) To effectuate social reform, according to Dewey, these three 'generative conditions' need to work together in ongoing, recursive cycles. This then, according to the American political scientist Christopher Ansell, results in 'evolutionary learning'. Ansell, one of the latest in a succession of scholars who are inspired by Dewey's pragmatism, describes the pragmatist theory of social reform as follows:

> Pragmatism departs from the strictly positivist view of experimentation by emphasizing the provisional, probative, creative and jointly constructed character of social experimentation. Pragmatism acknowledges the uncertainty and ambiguity inherent in problems and the partial perspectives we bring to bear on them. The results of inquiry are treated as fallible and, therefore, as provisional. Recognition of uncertainty and ambiguity leads to a probative stance: much of what inquiry does is to structure and define problems in such a way that we can make progress on them. (Ansell, 2011, 12–13)

Ansell argues that experimentation in this sense is a kind of 'dramatic rehearsal, in which possible lines of action are imagined and tentatively evaluated'. He also emphasises the importance of symbolic mediation in this process; the availability of concepts and stories that mediate the process of inquiry (Ansell, 2011, 13). Differently put, we need a vision, an ideal, to guide the process of reformist policy making.[2]

An example of such a guiding vision is provided by the British public intellectual and climate activist George Monbiot. He argues that neoliberalism, despite its extremist character and obvious devastating effects for ordinary working people, became such a powerful social ideology because it tells a simple story. That story is the well-known narrative of the power of the market as a simple, superior design for the coordination of productive human activity, liberty, opportunity, the heroic entrepreneur and the oppressive state with its self-seeking bureaucrats (Monbiot, 2017, 5; see also Chapter 6). To dislodge a successful story, it is not enough to criticise it; it needs to be replaced with another story. Monbiot's alternative story is one of 'hope and restoration'. It reveals the 'defining aspects of our nature' and seeks to 'revive our humanity'. Monbiot's reimaging of our society revolves around the following themes: 'the longing for belonging', 'good fellowship', the creation of a new commonwealth, democratic ownership, 'the wisdom of crowds', and 'coming home to ourselves'. This is not wishful thinking according to Monbiot. His alternative story draws on 'experience, action and practical possibility' (Monbiot, 2017, 182–186; see also Purdy, 2019).

The pragmatist conception of social reform shows remarkable similarities with an image of human nature that is common in utopian thinking. Instead of delineating a list of traits, states or capacities that are central to human flourishing, utopian thinkers think of human nature as the capacity for becoming. Where adversity and oppression can stifle any human property or capacity, it cannot suppress the imaginative urge to design a better world. 'This capacity for becoming – for developing in a host of different ways, and for acquiring new skills and dispositions – is a striking feature of human nature.' (Sayer, 2011, 114) An unexpected example of this irrepressible spirit of becoming and reinvention can be found among the nomads of contemporary American capitalism. These older citizens, as we have seen in Chapter 1, were forced out of their middle class existence into a transient life of occasional employment through the loss of their home, pension and the incursion of crippling debt often because of large medical bills. Yet, they develop a tribal spirit that is at the same time subversive and uplifting. As journalist Jessica Bruder says about one of the American nomads she encountered in her journeys to document this new phenomenon: 'He suggests that "van-dwellers" are conscientious objectors from a broken, corrupting social order. Whether or not they choose their lifestyle, they embrace it' (Bruder, 2017, 204). Bruder quotes a Facebook posting of another of the nomads, travelling from short-term job to short-term job in their recreational vehicles (RV):

> I can't decide if it's sad or hopeful that SO MANY of the folks I talk to in my various RV groups are going full-time because of financial hardship. I suppose it is bittersweet. The new freedom ... able to live while reinventing oneself. Thank goodness for the deep and varied Tribes out there that offer so much guidance, advice, stuff, and willing ears. Is this the evolution of the former middle class? (Bruder, 2017, 176, capitals in original)

Bruder concludes: 'The truth as I see it is that people can both struggle and remain upbeat simultaneously, through even the most soul-testing of challenges. This does not mean they are in denial. Rather, it testifies to the remarkable ability of humankind to adapt, to seek meaning and kinship when confronted with adversity.' (2017, 164–165) It is in this utopian spirit of joint practical discovery, creation, kinship and revaluation, in the face of overwhelming odds against progressive social change, that we want to approach public infrastructure, and the other topics of this book.

Perhaps it seems that we have drifted away from the subject of this chapter, ensuring a comprehensive and well-functioning public infrastructure. The nature of our human predicament (complexity and hegemony) and the enormity of the challenges that have been laid bare by the COVID-19 pandemic compel us to think beyond piecemeal reform. If we are to improve systematic exclusion, confront political nihilism and reverse climate destruction, we need comprehensive reforms. Public infrastructure is one element of such reform. Housing, good government, real corporate responsibility and a new understanding of money and its role in society are other essential building blocks of comprehensive reform. They are held together in a process of evolutionary learning by a strong and continuously evolving vision of a better society.

Our conclusion is that good and extensive public infrastructures are a necessary condition for the functioning of internally networked societies as well as for the kind of cooperation needed for the resolution of global problems. Modern societies and production processes are far too complex to be left to the devices of 'the market'. (The same applies to modern production processes – despite the fact that businesses, as we will see, deny their dependency on adequate public infrastructure.) This is not only a functional argument but also a moral one. Institutional solidarity – that is, institutions that allocate goods, entitlements and duties based on needs and capabilities, and not on ability to pay – is an important value in itself. In fact, we will later see that the elements of public infrastructure closely correspond to the needs that Green (New) Deal plans identify as the basis for a sufficient, humane existence. Adequate public infrastructure is a form of public wealth that makes an equal and just society possible. Public infrastructure is a moral good that benefits everyone.

4

Housing is a public good, not a commodity

In Chapter 3 we outlined the importance of a comprehensive, well-funded public infrastructure that includes essential public services. We believe that housing is, if not the most important item on this list, the foundation for almost everything else.

In an exhibition about poverty in the 19th and early 20th century in the Wien Museum in Vienna (Schwartz et al, 2007), we saw old black and white movie reels about working class housing in the United Kingdom just after the First World War. Whole families in one grimy unheated room, one toilet and water outlet for dozens of families in the courtyard, and heart-breaking stories of eviction. The situation was similar or worse in Vienna at the time, as we will see below. During the First World War, the Emperor had to intervene when his soldiers defected en masse on discovering that their families were evicted from their homes back in Vienna. (He introduced the tenant protection legislation that is still in effect today.) The documentary also contained interviews with people who had moved to newly built public housing with running water, an inhouse toilet, and two rooms and a kitchen. To witness, across the chasm of history, the gratification of these families with their new living quarters was a moving experience. It was clear from their stories that the improved quality of their new dwelling somehow enhanced their dignity. For the first time in their life, they said, they had a secure and stable home. Since those hard times, Vienna and the UK followed different trajectories. We can learn a lot about public housing by taking a closer look at them.

The UK: housing as a frontier of rentier capitalism

As everywhere else, housing has been a political issue in the UK for over a century. Until the 1970s, it read like a success story: in 1920, 576 housing units were built by local authorities. This number rose to 120,000 before the Second World War. Interrupted by the

Second World War, efforts to increase the stock of affordable housing resumed in the postwar era. In 1946, 25,000 new housing units were completed, and the number increased gradually until 1953, when the peak of almost 230,000 new units per year was reached. Until the 1970s, the figure remained consistently above 100,000 new units per year, only to plummet abruptly at the same time as the 'Right to Buy' was introduced by the Thatcher government in 1980. In 2003, only 286 residential units were completed, which is half the number of completed housing units in the 1920s (Merret, 1979 and Wilcox quoted in Jones and Murie, 2006, 19). Clearly, central and local governments no longer considered the public construction of affordable housing a priority, a responsibility of the state towards its citizens. The explanation is that in this period housing, and the whole ecosystem that supports domestic construction, as well as the discourse and collective imagination regarding housing, was de facto privatised. Housing became a responsibility of individual citizens.

What explains this drastic change? Perhaps the change was not so abrupt in the first place. Thatcher's Right to Buy scheme was not so much a break with the past but the culmination, or realisation, of a long tradition in British conservative politics: the property-owning democracy. Since the 1920s British Conservatives had been looking to safeguard the stability of the political order from the twin threats of liberalism and socialism that followed from the introduction of the franchise – and, further on the horizon, the alleged threat of the Russian Revolution. A fairer and more equal distribution of property would create a closer allegiance of an educated franchise to the capitalist production system. The Conservative Noel Skelton, who coined the term 'property-owning democracy', argued that '[p]rivate property has an ethical value and it is also essential to stability since possession brings "an increased sense of responsibility, a wider economic outlook, a practical medium for the expression of moral and intellectual qualities"' (Skelton, 1924, in Ron, 2008, 174). Note that in this context, property-owning refers to *individual* property, namely property held by individual citizens or families, and not by cooperatives or by the public. As we will see in Chapter 6, in the decades after the Second World War the political-economic order took a turn towards welfare statism. Nevertheless, the individualistic version of a 'property-owning democracy' continued to enjoy great popularity among Conservative politicians. Anthony Eden famously called for a 'nation-wide property-owning democracy' in his 1946 speech to the Conservative party conference, and throughout the 1950s it remained a staple of Tory party manifestoes (Ron, 2008,

177). Thatcher's Right to Buy programme was, thus, a continuation of longstanding Conservative ideas about the proper organisation of the political-economic order, and concurred with the Conservative drive to emasculate the welfare state.

As always, when dealing with policy, it is important to distinguish between policy on paper and policy in practice. Ron sensibly points out that in practice it makes a big difference if the emphasis is on *property* or *democracy* in the phrase 'property-owning democracy', and shows that in practice 'property' usually takes precedence (Ron, 2008, 170).[1] This is not necessary *only* the result of ideological preference. Every policy needs to make the transition from intention to realisation. In practice the foremost assets to which property rights are held are land and housing. (And nowadays equity. We will return to that in Chapter 8.) In an increasingly urbanised society it is plausible that housing will be the main means of property redistribution. But the effective distribution of privately owned housing in a mass society requires a carefully calibrated ecosystem of banks, tax laws, rent regulation (or rather the absence of it), building societies, real estate agencies, ad agencies and media that all work towards the same goal: to persuade citizens that buying their home is the sensible thing to do, and to make that ambition possible. One way to interpret British postwar housing policy is as the wilful emergence of this propertied ecosystem – including the financial instruments that enabled individual home ownership.

Also for this reason, this process is also one of an encroaching financialisation of housing. Financialisation means that economic value is increasingly realised through financial products, and not through trade or production in the real economy.[2] For example, when a car company whose main business model is to sell cars, starts to make a good proportion of its profits through mortgages or leasing contracts, then this is an instance of financialisation. What worries analysts of financialisation is that it seems to be an unstoppable process. The logic of finance invades and takes over ever more areas of society, and even our personal lives. Services that were traditionally provided through the public sector – think of care, higher education, old age pensions, public libraries – now have to be bought on the market from commercial vendors. Financialisation has increased the debts of private households.[3] It has forced organisations that operate in the public sector, such as housing associations, care facilities and universities, to change their business models to be able to borrow money from global investment banks (Smyth et al, 2020, 8). Social and economic justice, and the public interest are made subservient to financial objectives.

At the same time, financialisation would not have been possible without the active support, perhaps enablement is a better word, of the state. By reducing direct outlays for financing public services, introducing subsidies to make privatisation possible and creating complex arrangements of government departments, semi-public agencies, financial intermediaries (consultants, brokers, legal services) and investors, each of whom charge hefty fees for their services, a large chunk of public service delivery is now privatised. Privatisation is rarely cheap.

In the housing market, financialisation manifests itself, for example, in the transformation of building societies from commons working for the good of their members to limited companies aiming to maximise shareholder value – a transformation that mirrored the transfiguration of values, ambition and collective self-image of our society at large. For a century and half, building societies were, with housing associations and local councils, the three pillars of affordable housing in the UK. Local councils demonstrated the beneficial role of the state in the production of valuable social goods. Building societies were cooperative enterprises: local, communal, non-profit, based on cooperation, solidarity, risk-pooling and collective self-rule. Every town and city had a building society. They belonged to the institutional landscape of a community. Using the capital from monthly membership fees, they constructed affordable residential housing and gave members access to low interest loans to finance the purchase of a house. Building societies understood the needs of the community. They formed a national network, a socially minded cartel, regulated by the Chief Registrar of Friendly Societies. The state supported building societies via tax exemptions in exchange for controlling lending. There was capital involved, lots of it (£360 billion in 2008), but it was egalitarian, 'patient' capital working for the people, not the fast money of financial highflyers. Building societies were a perfect example of associative democracy (see Chapter 10). In contrast with the cultivation of privatised value, as in schemes for a property-owning democracy, early building societies offered members public control over investments and thus were manifestations of participatory democracy. They were local voluntary associations, to whom public power to manage an important societal sector had been devolved, regulated by a common framework of rules and financially supported by the state (Hirst, 1994, 33).

From a historical perspective, the UK housing system, like most of British society, was precariously balanced between a socialist-communal and conservative-individualistic impulse. Two developments changed this arrangement. The first was the electoral triumph of Thatcher, and the second the deregulation of banks. We will return to banking deregulation in Chapter 8; here we just note that driven by a crude free market ideology the state relinquished its control over the quantity of credit and its qualitative allocation (Ryan-Collins et al, 2011, 51). In this climate of aggressive financial entrepreneurism and tantalisingly high rewards for financial managers, building societies began to look anachronistic and wanted a piece of the pie. They began to relinquish their cooperatives roots and organise themselves like regular banks, a process called 'demutualisation'. By exchanging their mutual rights for shares, members became shareholders of the new bank. Using their housing and human capital accumulated in their years as small, local, voluntary associations, building societies morphed into consolidated all-purpose banks competing in the giddy world of global finance.

This climate of individualism and risk-taking, alongside the glorification of the free market, unleashed the pent-up energy of the Conservatives' individualistic property-owning ideology. In its simplest terms, Thatcher's Right to Buy policy offered tenants of council housing the possibility of buying their home. To make this offer attractive to people who might be apprehensive to take on a large amount of debt, the property was offered at a considerable discount. After a hesitant start it was a big success – in a narrow, instrumental sense. During the 1980s every year about 150,000 houses moved from the rental into the home-owner sector. Between 1980 and 2003 through the Right to Buy scheme 2.5 million units were taken out of the affordable housing sector, while only 672,000 units were built (McCall et al, 2020, 226). But the Right to Buy scheme would become a textbook example of what the American policy scholar Aaron Wildavsky half seriously called 'the Law of Large Solutions'. It implies 'that the greater the proportion of the population involved in a policy problem, and the greater the proportion of the policy space occupied by a proposed solution, the harder it is to find a solution that will not become its own worst problem' (1979, 63).

Politics and class are never far away in British policy making. Subsequent analyses of the Right to Buy scheme found that it contained a distinct class bias. The new owner-occupiers were predominantly white, in full-time work, usually holding manual skilled or white-collar occupations, and lived in households with more than one wage-earner. The Right to Buy scheme was also an attempt at taking control over housing policy away from local, particularly Labour dominated councils. Westminster simply cut the funding for affordable home construction of local councils. In 2010 councils were encouraged to freeze council tax (Crewe, 2016). The effect on council housing was disastrous. Although construction by councils did not decline at first, it did eventually to levels that were last seen in the 1920s, as we saw above. In a diminishing pool, council rents increased by over 50 per cent. The renters were in effect subsidising the discount for the Right to Buyers (Beckett, 2015). Moreover, many sitting tenants sold their newly acquired property to investors to be added to the barely regulated, overpriced, private rental stock (Christophers, 2019, 25).

A comparable story of government withdrawal and exposure to international financial markets can be told about housing associations. With their roots in occupational cooperative structures or philanthropy, non-profit housing associations first benefitted from direct funding for home construction but began to encounter a hostile environment in the austerity era after the financial crisis of 2008. The Conservative government implemented deep cuts in up-front capital funding and social grants for the construction of social housing. At the same time, it reclassified housing associations (HAs) as private sector bodies, freeing them, according to the Housing Secretary, 'from the shackles of public sector bureaucracy' so they could 'concentrate on their core, crucial business – building homes' (quoted in Smyth and Cole, 2019, 18). With lending by banks (the traditional source of capital for HAs) restricted after the crisis, HAs had little choice but to turn to international bond markets to fund their capital needs. In 2017, 58 housing cooperatives issued bonds worth a total of over £17 billion (Smyth et al, 2020, 3). And credit rating agencies increasingly assumed the role of a 'gateway constructor' (Smyth et al, 2020, 5), namely to decide for what purposes money is made available to whom and at what price; a role that was originally played by the state (and Chief Registrar of Friendly Societies). (We will say more about this in Chapter 8.) Financialisation shifts political power from democratically elected structures to for-profit companies with no or very little public accountability.

As urban geographer Aalbers notes, it is important to acknowledge that financialisation is not something that happens 'against' the state, or 'against' people. The state facilitates, and even drives, it, not only by providing the regulatory framework that allows financialisation, but also by 'pushing families into housing debt, by enabling financial institutions to buy up subsidised housing, or by simply withdrawing from providing or regulating the housing sector and opening up the field to rent-seeking financial institutions' (Aalbers, 2016, 4). Finance is increasingly becoming 'decoupled from production to become an independent power, an autocrat over the real economy' (Cox, 1992, 29, quoted in Aalbers, 2016, 41). In Aalbers' words, this market no longer pretends to produce anything: 'It is a market designed only to make money.' (Aalbers, 2016, 42) We will return to this important trend in Chapter 8 where we discuss the financial sector. But in everyday terms it means that people, willingly or not, have become cogs in the machinery of financialisation.

The geographer Brett Christophers argues that the financialisation of housing in the UK signifies a broader, more fundamental trend: the transformation of the country into a rentier economy. This is an important process that is not restricted to the UK, and as we will encounter it again in the chapters to come, we will briefly discuss some of its defining features. Christophers describes rent as 'income derived from the ownership, possession or control of scarce assets and under conditions of limited or no competition' (2019, 2). There is a heterodox understanding of rent, an understanding that concurs with our current neoliberal political economy, that is packed into this definition. Traditionally, rent is extracted from existing assets such as land or housing. Someone owns a scarce resource, others wish to use it, the owner charges a user fee. What is scarce or not is not hardwired into nature, however. As Karl Polanyi showed in his seminal book *The Great Transformation* (2001 [1944]), many resources that were once available to the community were made scarce by a process of enclosure. Charging user fees or rents for a resource that was once freely available under the stewardship of a community can be seen as the business model of modern capitalism.

By expanding the notion of rent, neoliberal capitalism has added a crucial innovation to rent extraction. Instead of rent being tied to a (scarce) often immobile asset, it is now defined by the ability of players in the market to stifle competition. Christophers calls it market power – specifically the power to monopolise an asset *and* milk it for financial gain (2019, 5). Think of internet giants such as Google or Amazon who use their monopoly position to extract our personal data which they then sell to advertisers. Perhaps it does not feel like extraction, but if you want to browse the internet or buy something online, you often have no choice but to deliver your personal details to these data behemoths.

The example demonstrates two aspects of modern rentier capitalism. The first is that it introduces an element of excess into the notion of rent extraction. Most of us have no problem accepting that an entrepreneur derives a good income from their business in a situation of market competition. We see it as a just reward for more clever innovation, better client relations, or higher quality products. Rent, however, is income that goes beyond competitive earnings, 'payments not justified by the requirements of an efficient economy' (Christophers, 2019, 5). These are not abstract musings of social theorists. Think of the CEO who 'earns' 278 times the average income of an employee in his firm (Mishel and Wolfe, 2019). The excess is the difference between his current income and what he would be willing to work for in more fair and competitive circumstances. For example, the 20 to 1 income ratio was common in 1965; a time in which we also had successful and innovative businesses.

The second aspect of contemporary rentier capitalism is the diversification of assets that can be corralled for monopolistic value extraction. Christophers helpfully lists them for us. The first are the classical rent-bearing assets of finance and land. What is new about them are the expanded opportunities to use them for rent extraction. These depend on complex legal and regulatory arrangements, as we have seen above. Natural resources (oil, gas, coal, metals) are a second category. The ability for rent extraction depends on ownership and leasing arrangements. In the latter case, a country that owns the resource enters into a lease arrangement with a private company that extracts the resource in return for a percentage of the proceeds. These arrangements can extend over many decades. Intellectual property (patents, copyrights) and spectrum assets (the right to exploit a particular electromagnetic frequency for communication purposes) are two more categories. And finally, he mentions platform, natural monopoly and contract rents. The latter are interesting as they cover the large area of contracting out and public-private arrangements through which public services are delivered in the UK. We will discuss them in Chapter 6.

The housing sector has been a vanguard in the transformation of the UK, and to a lesser extent the Northern European economies, into a rentier economy. While the UK is the poster child of this development, from the perspective of the average middle class citizen or the young generation the current housing landscape looks dismal in all these countries. Housing prices and rents in many cities are prohibitive, while affordable council-provided housing is exceedingly scarce. In the UK, between 1975 and 2014 the per capita completion of housing units was the lowest of six large European countries (Aubrey, 2015). The price/square metre ratio in the UK is the highest in Europe. More than 12.5 per cent of people in the United Kingdom spend 40 per cent or more of their disposable income on housing (Nardelli and Applegate, 2017). Due to sky-high rents in the private sector the United Kingdom spends far more on housing benefits than other European countries; 1.4 per cent of GDP as compared to about 0.1 per cent in Germany

(Aubrey, 2015). Housing costs have increased even more for low income families. Housing costs for people who earn about £16,000 a year increased by 45 per cent between 2010 and 2016, compared with an average rise of 10 per cent for the lowest earners across Europe (Booth, 2018). It is no surprise that in 2018 rough sleeping was 165 per cent higher in England than in 2010. Whatever statistic one chooses to use, homelessness and precarious housing have increased since 2010 (Fitzpatrick et al, 2019).

Perhaps more importantly, many UK citizens cannot imagine another kind of housing market. For-purchase housing has become an essential element of the economy. In the 2010s, property values accounted for more than 60 per cent of total British assets, or £4 trillion (other estimates even speak of £5.6 trillion; see Dorling, 2015, 2). The national media report on rising housing prices with the same breathless enthusiasm as a victory of the national football squad. The incorporation of housing policy into a complex system of financial markets has meant that it is no longer a service promoted by the British state to provide adequate housing for everyone, but a part of the global capitalist economic order, in which capital ownership has to yield ever greater returns. The British and US housing system also demonstrate the gap between the ideal and reality of the property-owning democracy. In many ways George W. Bush's 'ownership society' is the logical endpoint for the property-owning democracy. The laws, regulations and institutions that are required to implement the idea of a property-owning democracy inevitably moved it further and further away from its ideals of justice, fairness and democracy and towards the harsh environment of a highly unequal, laissez-faire housing market, propped up by feeble social support and periodical massive financial intervention. But there are alternatives that result in a fairer, more equitable, secure and humane housing situation for all. For this we travel to the continent.

Vienna: a century of integrative housing policy

Let us, by way of comparison, take a look at Vienna. Vienna is considered the world's capital of social housing. About 60 per cent of the housing stock in the Austrian capital qualifies as public housing. It is purpose built social housing that is publicly owned or built by a non-profit corporation, or social housing owned and run by a cooperative. In the latter category, people have to buy into the cooperative and then get an unlimited tenancy contract with low rent. Sometimes there is also the option to buy the flat that one is renting after a certain period. People who make use of this option subsequently have a cap on the rent they can ask from prospective tenants, as well as restrictions on how much they can sell it for. For privately owned houses built before 1945, the law prescribes rent ceilings, depending on the quality of the housing unit, its location, and a few other parameters. Rent controls are also in place for any other properties built with public funding. If tenants are offered a fixed-term rather than an open-ended lease (minimum three, commonly five years), then the rent must be cut by 25 per cent. In addition, in the public and non-profit sector, only open-ended leases are allowed. Recently, policy makers have suggested that even in the private sector, only permanent leases should be allowed, unless a private landlord can credibly claim to need a flat or house for themselves in the foreseeable future. While this proposal has not found a political majority yet, it demonstrates the kinds of measures that are considered to tackle the rise of housing costs in recent years. Moreover, to fight speculation, Austrian law imposes a tax of 30 per cent on real estate profits – unless the person selling it has lived in the property themselves and the property does not exceed a certain size.

Viennese public housing rests on five integrated policy measures which together are referred to as the 'Vienna Model' (Ludwig, 2017). First, active social protection organised around the availability of high quality, affordable housing and strict tenant protection laws. An interesting feature of public housing in Vienna is that it is not only for the lowest income strata. Eligibility criteria have been set such that 75 per cent of the Viennese population is eligible for public housing. Also, when a family's income rises, or when the children move out, people are not required to vacate their house, or move into a smaller home. This social mixing is a deliberate measure to prevent the stigmatisation of public housing. Second, Vienna pursues a proactive land purchase and zoning policy. The city uses its ability to invest in land while it is still affordable, without the necessity to immediately develop it, something that private developers cannot afford. The third element is a multi-pronged finance policy that consists of affordable rents, capped construction and land purchase costs, rent control, long amortisation periods, and earmarked income generation via loans to developers. The fourth element is to work with reliable, longstanding partners (predominantly housing corporations) who agree to a cap on profits (3.5 per cent of invested capital) and an obligation to reinvest capital in the construction of public housing. And finally, the city has a focus on innovation and managed competition in architecture, construction and sustainability (Ludwig, 2017).

Vienna's housing policy is a continuation of the philosophy and practices that were developed in the period between 1919 and 1934 – known as Red Vienna (*das Rote Wien*) – when a Social-Democratic administration developed an innovative, integrated and highly successful public housing policy. Both within Austria and internationally the breadth, depth and durability of the administrative, architectural and visionary achievements of Red Vienna have intrigued generations of scholars and commentators and has been the subject of numerous books, articles and exhibitions. The boldness and visionary quality of its public housing projects have inspired architects nationally and internationally (Blau, 1999). There is a general consensus that Vienna's current high quality of living is directly related to the achievements of the Red Vienna period. The Austrian historian Wolfgang Maderthaner calls Red Vienna 'one of the most extraordinary, creative and courageous communal experiments in modern European history' (2019, 24). This is all the more astonishing as the Social-Democratic administration of Red Vienna only lasted 15 years, operated in an increasingly hostile political environment, and faced a series of momentous challenges at its inception.

Before the era of Red Vienna, the housing situation in Vienna for the working class was downright disastrous. Substandard quality, lack of sanitation, overcrowding and excessive rents defined working class housing. Evictions were the order of the day. Social pathologies such as alcoholism and domestic violence were rampant. The working class districts were regularly affected by epidemics of lethal infectious diseases such as cholera, typhoid fever, smallpox and the common flu. Tuberculosis was so common that it was called the '*morbus Viennensis*'. At the end of the First World War, Austria found itself on the side of the defeated. The new city administration faced enormous challenges. During the Great War an unending stream of refugees from the outlying parts of the Habsburg Empire had descended upon the city. This had stretched an already disastrous housing situation to the breaking point, so that at the time of the armistice in November 1918 hundreds of thousands of people were living in miserable, substandard living quarters, tens of thousands were homeless, hygienic conditions were catastrophic, resulting in frequent and deadly epidemics and acute food shortages. In the immediate aftermath of the war Austria suffered both economic collapse and hyperinflation, and the city's finances were at an all-time low. How did the Social-Democratic city administration manage to turn this situation around?

In an article that one of us (HW) wrote with the Austrian historian Florian Wenninger, the authors show that the administration's remarkable achievements were the result of a three-pronged approach: a vigorous construction programme, creative financing with an emphasis on progressive taxation, and a coherent, integrative vision which the authors characterise as 'progressive humanism': an open-ended, holistic, forward-looking, utopian vision of the place of the working class in urban society. The administration's progressive vision to improve the physical, mental and educational condition of the working classes fulfilled three functions. It guided the administration's integrative policy making, it mobilised societal groups, such as unions, women's organisations, and idealistic young doctors, to contribute to the administration's efforts and it attracted competent public figures, architects and artists who were not necessarily socialists to work for the administration (such as its finance minister Hugo Breitner, who was a banker; see Wagenaar and Wenninger, 2020).

Wagenaar and Wenninger summarise the achievements of Red Vienna as follows:

> Housing programs existed in many cities and states during the inter-war period – but what made the case of Vienna so special, apart from the way it was financed, was the fact that, in the course of their planning and construction, residential buildings became places with multiple functions thanks to numerous public authorities and influential groups working closely together, including the Social Democratic party in the narrower sense. They reflected an extraordinarily dynamic municipal reform program that, in addition to providing high-quality and affordable housing, included five other cornerstones: care, education, health policy, adult education and cultural policy (Kofler, 2004, 53). In this sense, the community buildings were not only places of living, but of community development, social engineering and political awareness work. (2020, 428)

The physical achievements of Red Vienna, the architecturally ambitious public housing blocks, are still in use and can be admired today (Blau, 1999). But Red Vienna's true legacy is less visible to the public eye. It consists of a template and a culture. The template is the set of policy principles and practices – forward-looking, integrative, organised around patient capital, and aimed at the public interest – that still today define Vienna's housing policy (Ludwig, 2017). The culture is an attitude of care for the quality of life in the city and inclusiveness for all that infuses the city administration.

Having said this, Vienna has not been immune to the forces of global capital. Financialisation, privatisation and speculation are working their way into the Viennese housing sector. Very little new social housing has been built since 2004, when the city of Vienna switched its focus from building and renting out public housing to supporting cooperatives. Throughout the 2010s, the ratio of privately financed and publicly funded construction of new housing projects reversed: in 2008, about 20 per cent of building permits were given in the privately financed sector, and 80 per cent in the public one. By 2017, about 70 per cent of new housing projects were privately funded. It is an effect also of the fact that Vienna has increasingly become a target of private investors, big and small. Displacement is eating away at the inclusionary composition of the population of Vienna that gives the city its lively and relaxed character. The major beneficiaries of this development are, as everywhere else, banks and developers. Banks finance the developers, the construction companies, and then also the private and corporate buyers. Rents in the private sector, although still regulated, are tentatively liberalised. Landlords can now add a 'location premium' to the rent and many do not apply the 25 per cent reduction on short-term leases. As a result, rents are rising, although, depending on location, still far below the levels of London, Paris or Amsterdam.

We use Vienna as an example here not only, but also, because we live here, and we know it well. After many years of living in in other cities, including Amsterdam and London, we moved to Vienna in 2017 where we now rent a flat – very affordable and with a kind of lease that is unbreakable by the (private) landlord – and where nobody frowns upon people who rent. We are conscious of our privileged situation; in other parts of the world (including other parts of Austria; Vienna is unique in this respect), housing has become a commodity. Our relocations have also made us aware of the fragility of affordable housing. Berlin is a demonstration case.

Long a haven of affordable housing, in the 1990s, legal changes were introduced that allowed private landlords to charge 'market-conform' rents after a tenant had moved out. The results were predictable. Thousands of tenants were bribed or pressured to give up their affordable lease to allow the property owner to double or triple the rent. Simultaneously Berlin became a Walhalla for property developers, who were given free rein by the city administration, and housing prices began to rise rapidly. Within a few years much of Berlin was out of reach for low and middle-income families, and 'displacement and eviction [had] become a routine experience for many Berliners' (Vasudevan, 2020). Thanks to a culture of unyielding and vocal protest and active citizen participation, the current Red-Green coalition passed a cap on rents and introduced fines for landlords who exceed the caps. The rent cap has put a halt to the 'displacement economy' that the Berlin rental market had become, but, important as it is, it does not change the fact that the city lacks an integrative housing and social welfare policy. As the urban sociologist Andrej Holm argues: 'The rent moratorium does not change anything about the fundamental situation of housing shortage, land speculation and gaps in social welfare policy' (2019, translation by authors).

Holm's article contains a number of further valuable lessons. The rent cap has led to the usual chorus of protest from the real estate lobby, which claims that it will result in an investment 'strike' and stifle investment in housing. It also suggests that rent caps violate the rights of real estate developers. And, an argument that is particularly pertinent in Berlin, one only need to bring back to memory the sorry state of housing in the former German Democratic Republic to have a showcase example of the effects of state-owned real estate. Holm counters this alarmist rhetoric of real estate lobbies with a set of sober calculations. Even a rent as low as €4 per square metre, he shows, is sufficient for landlords to cover maintenance and service costs; everything else is just rentierism. There is no better illustration of the hold that the hegemony about high housing costs has on our collective consciousness than the protests lodged by housing associations against the rent cap. They calculate that they would lose €500 million during the five-year rent cap; money that cannot be used for the construction of affordable housing. Holm dismisses this as a rhetorical trope: the crushingly large number that kills all debate. He shows that this would indeed result in a reduction of 1,000 houses per year. But if all rent increases by housing associations would be used for new housing construction – a big 'if' in the current financialised environment – it would cover 4,000 houses per year. What Berlin needs is 20,000 new units per year, a volume that cannot possibly be financed through rent increases. It requires generous public funding and the kind of integrative approach that the city of Vienna uses, for example.

Our vision: a housing guarantee

Housing is a hybrid of bricks and dreams. A home forms a flashpoint for our aspirations and fears; a storehouse of meaning, strong attachments and intense memories. In sociological terms it is an object of personal expression and status differentiation. At the same time housing is an object of cold speculation, one of the frontiers of financialised capitalism. At its fundamental level it is a basic necessity; what social scientists call a 'condition of possibility' of living. Housing is simultaneously focalised and dispersed. It is that one apartment or house to which we hold the key, and it is a dispersed ecosystem of banks, mortgage lenders, real estate agencies, valuators, notaries, lawyers and advertisement agencies. It is also a discourse that permeates society and our individual consciousness.

In London, where we lived for a decade before moving to Vienna, the price of housing is a popular topic at middle class dinner parties. One of the most bizarre phenomena is the breathless media celebration of rising housing prices. To buy your own house, to obtain equity, is the central aspiration of many young couples, and they are willing to take on unsustainable levels of debt for that. Housing has become a token of social class. If you are unable to get 'onto the property ladder', you are considered a second-class citizen. These young people are not to blame. Buying a home is often the only way to get access to stable housing. And it is fed by the – often erroneous – belief that this chunk of brick and mortar will protect you and your family from the vagaries of the market. Often it does not. Those who are forced to – literally – buy into the market are much more vulnerable to its volatilities than those who opt out.

So far, what this chapter has shown are two contrasting social philosophies of housing provision: the property-owning democracy versus welfare statism. In a way the developments described in this (very broad-brush) overview reflect a natural experiment in national housing policy. In terms of equality, security and housing quality, welfare statism 'wins' hands down. The problem with the property-owning democracy is that, by necessarily delegating the financing and construction of housing to private companies, it exposes the provision of housing to market forces, to the imperative of banks and construction companies to turn a profit. By triggering destructive processes of financialisation and rentierism it is exposed more to the law of large solutions than its alternative. The property-owning democracy is unable to mitigate the externalities of housing markets. In fact, the paradox of the property-owning democracy is that to make it work it requires strong state intervention – exactly the thing that conservative social philosophers seek to avoid.[4] The problem with welfare state housing policy, as the Berlin examples show, is its vulnerability to market forces, or rather corporations, banks, property owners and governments working in cahoots to capture and exploit the housing market. And it constrains the freedom to dispense with your property as you see fit – not a minor point for conservatives and market liberals.

Nevertheless, we side with the direct provision of housing by the state supported by strong tenant protection regulation. Housing does not need to, and should not, be commodified. People need not be forced to make large financial sacrifices that will keep the bank happy and make themselves overworked and sleepless for years or even decades to come. Renting your home does not make you a second-class citizen; with adequate tenant protection, it makes you a more autonomous and happier one. Instead of saving to buy a house, we should push for better tenant protection.

In our vision – foreshadowed in Chapter 3 where we argued that housing is a fundamental need of people and should be included in the services provided by the public – every person living in a country should be entitled to renting a housing unit of a given size, meaning a specific square footage at a specific building standard within an indicated region. The lease must be secure; that is, it cannot be dissolved as long as the tenant complies to the terms of the contract. The size of the home that people are entitled to should be determined for single households, with footage being added for every additional member of the household. The size per person can vary across different regions with less footage per person available in metropolitan centres than in rural regions. The rent – which should be established such that people with median incomes spend no more than a quarter of their monthly income on it – can vary between less and more sought-after regions. While citizens should have a right to indicate the region that they want to live in, housing authorities should have some leeway in assigning units to people as they are available – that is, our housing guarantee does imply the right to choose in what city or region one will live, but not necessarily in what specific neighbourhood.

While the right to housing should be independent of people's wealth and income, it should come with a requirement to live in that accommodation as one's sole place of residence; people with second homes (that they use for themselves) would thus be disqualified from applying. Moreover, while all leases would be open ended, people who buy a flat or house to live in would need to move out of their social housing unit. By this we seek to discourage buy-to-let ownership. At the same time, a housing guarantee would impose a positive duty on public authorities to ensure that sufficient high quality rental units are built to meet demand.

We do not argue that housing should never be for sale. But the ability to buy a home must not be a requirement for people to get access to affordable and stable housing. Banks should be regulated in that interest rates are reasonable, mortgage contracts transparent, and monthly payments never exceed a sustainable percentage of the lender's annual salary over the mortgage's term. (And, as we will see in Chapter 8, ideally, the banks are public banks.) Housing appraisal for the purpose of establishing the size of the mortgage should reflect the current use value of a house, not the expected future value on a fictitious housing market. These measures would automatically put a ceiling on housing prices. To protect against the intrusion of wealthy speculators, they should be required to demonstrate that they live in the house for a minimum of seven months a year. And profits from any sale of a flat or house that people have not lived in while it was in their possession should be levied by taxes high enough to make it unattractive to treat housing stock as an investment.

There is a lot of truth in the motto of 'housing first' that social work applies when supporting people with mental health or other issues. The right to shelter is a human right – and, to quote political scientist Louise Haagh, for the right to social security to be effective, it needs to be secure (2019).

5

Redefining work and income

The gradual destruction of the fair labour contract

In his book *Buying Time*, his astute analysis of the course of post-Second World War capitalism, the German political economist Wolfgang Streeck argues that at the end of the 1960s, business began to withdraw from the postwar social pact (Streeck, 2017) – the particular settlement between capital, labour and the state that had ushered in the welfare state and the *trentes glorieuses*, three decades of social stability and affluence for the many. We will tell this story more fully in the next chapter on good government. Streeck describes how the dissolution of the postwar settlement had enormous consequences for almost every aspect of the organisation of state, society and economy. One of its most prominent victims was the gradual destruction of the fair labour contract.

Over the last 50 years the share of the national income pie that went to labour has steadily decreased, while that of capital has increased. According to OECD figures, between 1975 and 2013 the share of labour in the national income declined from more than 65 per cent to 56 per cent (ILO and OECD, 2015). This simple figure masks massive, wrenching changes in the lives of workers. First, wages have stagnated. For example, in the United States, from 1979 to 2018, net productivity rose by 70 per cent, while the hourly pay of typical workers essentially stagnated – increasing only 12 per cent over 39 years (after adjusting for inflation). This means that productivity rose six times as much as wages in that period (EPI, 2019). The OECD shows a similar decoupling between productivity and wages across its 24 member states (although with considerable differences between states; Schwellnus et al, 2017).

Perhaps an even bigger change has been the gradual displacement of full-time, regularly paid and contractually formalised employment with 'non-standard employment'. The latter is a euphemism for situations where workers have a lot of responsibility, risk, and stress, low pay, and few, if any, rights. Until roughly the start of the new millennium, in the rich world, the majority of those who worked for money did so in full-time non-temporary, work secured by employment contracts with more or less generous benefits, union recognition, job protection, worker consultation, and protected by sector-wide wage negotiations. Today, many people only know this from the stories of their parents. Whole industries, such as the care sector, food retailing, hospitality and increasingly also universities, rely on people working in precarious jobs: zero-hour contracts, short-term employment, and all sorts of informal unregulated work at the bottom of the labour market.

This process of increasing precariousness in the labour market has different causes. The shift from a production to a service economy is one. The emergence of digital technologies as vehicles for commerce on the one hand and surveillance on the other is a second cause. Wage competition through offshoring, declining union membership, union suppression, and the relentless drive towards shareholder value also play a role. And, particularly in the Anglophone countries, government has played an active role in suppressing union activity and deregulating work contracts. This convergence of powerful technological, economic and administrative forces has made the rise of precarious work seem unstoppable. Non-standard employment, as precarious work relations are called in policy circles, is on the rise throughout the whole working world, with differences across regions and population groups (women and younger people are particularly affected in many countries; ILO, 2016). The business model of entire sectors, such as higher education or the care industry, relies on low wage work – as whole societies became painfully aware during the COVID crisis. Is this the end of work? Is this model of work sustainable?

What is work?

Let us take a step back and define what we mean by work. Across the rich world, people speaking of 'work' normally refer to paid work. There are many historical reasons for this: the Viennese historian Andrea Komlosy, in her impressive global history of work (2018), highlights the separation between the home and the workplace, a process that began with the industrial revolution at the start of the 19th century, as one of the reasons for this. People moved from rural areas to urban centres where factories were located. Rather than working on their farms or in workshops within their villages, people now went out of their homes to earn their livelihoods. What took place outside the home and brought in money was gainful labour – and this was typically performed by the head of the family, the husband and father.

Activities inside the house became the domain of the 'housewife', a term that in the Middle Ages stood for the head of a household community. In the 20th century, this significant and active social function degenerated into a collective term for a new, invisible groups: housewives were women who were 'only' at home, who 'did not work'. The unpaid toil of women (and many children) was not *real* work, it was not captured by economic metrics either: 'The reciprocal, the immediate and the gratuitous were pushed out of the economic sphere, devalued and banned from economic statistics so that their continued existence went unnoticed, and could be absorbed by the dominant modes of production and perception.' (Komlosy, 2018, 21) This narrow understanding of work, which travelled to many world regions through different forms of colonialism, also completely disregarded the social and economic value that resulted from work in the informal sector, which is where more than half of the world's population works. Against this backdrop it is important to keep in mind that the conflation of work with paid work that so many take for granted is specific to the western world of the last 100 years or so. Throughout much of human history, things have been different.

Seen from this perspective it is less surprising that a 2018 Opinion by the European Group on Ethics (EGE), an advisory group to the European Commission that one of us (BP) is a member of, set out to broaden the definition of work (EGE, 2018). In 2017, the (then) Commissioner for Research, Science and Innovation, Carlos Moedas, requested an Opinion by the EGE on the future of work. At that time, the elimination of people's jobs by processes of digitalisation and automation were hotly debated in newspapers and magazines. The consensus among economists and business pundits was that workers needed to upskill themselves to ensure that they remained competitive in the labour market.

From the start it was clear to us that this way if framing the future of work was problematic. The vision of robots taking over jobs rested on a number of assumptions that we believed were not only empirically wrong but also questionable in terms of the solutions they suggested. First, it implied that digitalisation and automation were the primary causes of the problem that we are grappling with. Rather than having created the problem, however, these processes have merely exacerbated it. The root cause was that we, as a society, had allowed it to happen that an increasing proportion of people can no longer obtain sufficient income from paid work to lead a dignified life. This applies not only to people who lost their jobs due to machines. It is also true for the large number whose job(s) do not give them enough income to pay for food, housing, transport and the education of their children. The situation that wages have not kept pace with productivity gains is one reason for this; the growth of precarious and badly paid employment is another. A third is hedonic inflation, meaning that the products and services that many people, in the rich world, use for daily living have increased in cost more than our income has. Cars, phones and housing cost more, partly because their quality improved (phones and computers), but partly also because they became increasingly commodified and commercialised (housing). In effect, we now spend a larger chunk of our incomes on these things, meaning that even high earners are often only one pay packet away from defaulting on their mortgage payments.

Another problematic assumption is that individual workers are held responsible for their own 'upskilling'. Even if we agree with the technology optimists that digitalisation and automation will, in the middle and long run, create more new jobs than they destroy, these new jobs will require skills that not everyone will be able to acquire. Not everybody is capable of becoming an online fitness trainer, a human shopping aide for the elderly or a software developer. From today's vantage point it looks very likely that, while those with the right kind of education, training and skill, will be able to choose from an ever-widening range of well-paid and meaningful jobs, other people will be permanently unemployable. No matter how hard they try, and how many incentives and workforce programmes are thrown at them, they will not be able to obtain the skills that the new labour market will need. It is ethically dubious to assume that it is people's individual responsibility to assure that they remain competitive in these circumstances. We are facing a future in which the market for paid work is such that it values only certain groups of people. The rest will be unemployable, or hop from one underpaid gig to the next, struggling to make ends meet.

It is both futile and unfair to hold people individually responsible for their own 'upskilling'. Society – in the form of the laws, policies and institutions that we have created that distribute rights and entitlements – has brought about the problem of the future of work that we are now trying to solve. Because our institutions are implicated in the current, precarious state of work, we need to solve it collectively. For this reason, the EGE Opinion on the Future of Work introduced the term of 'societal upskilling' as an antidote to the presumption that people are individually responsible for being competitive at the labour market. It means that society as a whole bears responsibility to ensure that every person can lead a dignified life. Doing so would require an adjustment of our political, social and economic institutions to the new forms and roles of work in our society. Attempting to expand the protections and rights attached to regular employment to atypical forms of work and employment will not suffice. We envisage two complementary strategies at this point. The first is to provide a democratic alternative to the governance of business enterprises by promoting and incentivising the distribution of the cooperative model throughout the economy. The second is a new social contract that entails a stronger decoupling of work and income. Both strategies support and strengthen each other.

Promote cooperatives

The literature on cooperatives is too large to discuss here, so we can only touch upon it. Cooperatives emerged in the 19th century in Germany in agriculture and banking (Raiffeisen) and the UK in retail and housing, as we saw in Chapter 4. They were member-based, self-organising associations that supported people by pooling resources and protecting them against the risks of poverty, famine and lack of capital (Birchall and Kettilson, 2009). From Germany they spread throughout Europe. During the Great Depression in the 1930s cooperatives sprang up in the United States, Canada and Sweden. Most people are not aware that today cooperatives are still widespread and generate almost 5 per cent of GDP in the G10 countries (Sanchez Bajo and Roelants, 2013, 105). Some large transnational enterprises, such as the Desjardins Cooperative group, a financial institution in Quebec (Desjardins, 2020), and the Mondragon industrial group in Spain, are cooperatives.

Cooperatives have governance structures and surplus distribution mechanisms that differ significantly from those of the public limited company that dominates the business landscape. Internal governance of cooperatives is not based on ownership but on democratic membership. Sanchez Bajo and Roelants define a cooperative as an 'association of persons (that) develops its activities through an enterprise that is jointly owned and democratically controlled in its entrepreneurial processes and activities' (2013, 116). Cooperatives thus combine associative and entrepreneurial principles of ownership and control. Employment cooperatives are organised around members' needs. According to Sanchez Bajo and Roelants, 'They herald a moral value system with such declared values as democracy, equality, equity, solidarity, honesty and social responsibility. They lay a strong emphasis on education and training and claim to be concerned with the community' (Sanchez Bajo and Roelants, 2013, 101). Cooperatives offer an opportunity to ordinary citizens to become trained in carrying entrepreneurial responsibilities and participate in economic democracy. The members of the Desjardin Group, for example, receive training to function on the boards of local credit boards. Within the environment in which they operate, cooperatives create a stakeholder economy. They take the needs and values of the community that they serve into account. We will see in Chapter 7 that corporate social responsibility is difficult to realise within the common shareholder model; stakeholder democracy is one of the key cooperative principles.

There is no principled reason why companies cannot be organised according to cooperative principles. They are not less profitable and more stable than public limited companies. They weather financial and economic crises better, and they are employment machines. In effect, national governments and international organisations such as the International Labour Organization that support cooperatives would achieve a number of important goals: establish adequate work contracts, promote workplace democracy, create a stakeholder economy, and promote sustainable investment. In Chapter 9 we will argue that the cooperative would be the ideal model for the green businesses that are an integral part of Green (New) Deal initiatives.

Broadening the notions of work and income

The second strategy is to loosen the tight coupling of work and income. Such an institutional reform to adjust to the new role and value of work would leave no domain of our economic and political life untouched. Education and training are an example. The tacit contract between employers and the rest of society is broken. The former used to pay workers enough to lead a decent life, while public institutions and public money educated and trained people so that employers can count on a skilled work force. But when certain types of companies increasingly 'employ' machines instead of people, and – starting long before the digital revolution – are paying their human employees so little in some sectors that people in full-time work do not have enough to live on, then the obligation of society to provide a skilled and willing work force has changed too.

Manufacturing is but the most extreme example: it has been in manufacturing that automation has advanced the most, and where many humans have already been replaced by machines. When companies use machines instead of humans to do the manufacturing, why does our education system still train people to do these jobs? Why do we not train people to get better in the things that are, thus far, uniquely human, that cannot be done by machines: compassion, critical and creative thinking, leading a good and meaningful life? Some visionaries have suggested that, instead of training people to work hard, we need to educate them how to be lazy. Leaving the provocative framing aside, there is some truth in this statement. Social status, and arguably also income, will increasingly come from work outside of employment. We thus need to teach our children and grandchildren how to be good citizens, and how to care for themselves and for others – and for the environment.

The first step that underpins such institutional reform is to broaden our understanding of work, as suggested by the EGE Opinion. The future of work that we envisage requires a more inclusive understanding of what counts as work. We all know how hard many people work who do not hold a paid job: people who look after children or sick relatives, people who train others in music or sports, who volunteer in community organisations. An approach that breaks up the anachronistic conflation of work with paid work defines work as everything that a third person can do for you. They can build a house, cook a meal, and help you with your personal hygiene if you are unable to do that yourself. They cannot, however, sleep or love or enjoy art for you.

Such a broad understanding of work leads to two possible courses of action. One, popular among feminists in the 1970s, is to suggest that, because a lot of currently unpaid work makes a major contribution to our society and economy, it needs to be recognised as formal work and remunerated fairly (Wezerek and Ghodsee, 2020; Wages for Housework, n.d.). The second is to decouple income from work and introduce a form of basic financial security for every person, a universal basic income (UBI). Many people, including many from the Left, look at UBI with suspicion. This is because UBI has recently been advocated by the right as a way to offload the responsibility of businesses for the welfare of their employees even further. While this has historically been an important concern, there is another tradition of designing UBI that does not hollow out the welfare state.

The bread-and-butter model of universal basic income

One of us (BP) has recently made her own contribution to the debate by making a case for UBI on the basis of human dignity and social solidarity (Prainsack, 2020b). She draws, among others, on the work of political scientist Louise Haagh, who argues that subsistence – namely having the necessary means to lead a dignified life – is a human right (2019). We assert that if this is to be more than an empty claim, societies have a moral obligation to acknowledge and enforce this right. And if we agree with the 'subsistence as a human right' stance, then it follows that the necessary means for people to lead a dignified life need to be provided to everyone unconditionally, and not only to people above a specific age, those without employment, the disabled, or any other specific group.

A considerable part of what is required for a dignified life is, and should be, provided via public services and infrastructures, as outlined in Chapter 3. For those needs that cannot, and should not, be met via public services, a UBI in the form of a universal, unconditional and individual basic income would be a very good solution. In Barbara's book, she proposes what she calls a bread-and-butter model of UBI (Prainsack, 2020b). The actual financial payment (the UBI in the narrow sense of the word) is the butter. But the butter needs to sit on something, the bread – and the bread are the public services and infrastructures that meet most of people's fundamental needs and enable them to partake in society. In this sense, our ideal system of basic social security consists of one element that is provided in the form of public services and infrastructure (the bread), and one that consists of income (the butter). We do not favour a neoliberal model of a UBI that replaces all social transfers and obliterates public service provision. Such a UBI that tells people 'take the money and shut up' is morally problematic. It also is not an effective corrective to the toxicity of the current world of work.

Such a solidaristic form of universal social security would not, as sometimes suggested by critics of UBI, be 'money for nothing'; a payment to people so that they do not need to work. On the contrary, it would be given to people as an acknowledgement of the contributions that they already make, or the contributions that they would be making if they had the time and opportunity. And as a sum of money that can help fuller participation in society. It is money that people get because they are human beings. And it would also arguably mitigate social fragmentation and pre-empt a further loss of solidarity within our societies. The gap, in terms of social status, stigma and wealth, between people in employment (or those who draw pensions as a result of their employment) and those who are un- or precariously employed is getting bigger. A UBI that grants everyone the right of subsistence due to their being a member of our society, regardless of how poor or rich, and how healthy or sick, they are, would emphasise what people have in common, and not what sets them apart. It would make it easier, we believe, for people to recognise each other as a fellow member of a community with a right to a dignified life, who is, as we all are, exposed to an unpredictable cocktail of risk and luck and tries her best to contribute.

And although it may, at first sight, not be 'fair' that rich people would also receive their monthly UBI payment, it should indeed be given to everyone. It is a matter of principle. It is something that all people would have in common, a universal protection against poverty in a given society. Those who do not need the financial support of a UBI because their incomes from work or wealth are high enough should contribute, in turn, via progressive income taxes and wealth taxes. In fact, most models for a solidaristic, emancipatory UBI envisage that the introduction of the latter should be accompanied by much higher taxes on wealth than in the current system.

Data from experiments with unconditional basic income all around the world (there are no studies with *universal* basic income in the sense that everyone in a given country received it) give us no reason to assume that, even with a generous UBI, people would work less. Some people may do different things than they do today – such as give up a job that they hate but have needed to hold on to in order to survive and look for something different. But there is no reason to expect that people would do fewer useful things. On the contrary, there are indications that the relationship between paid work on the one hand, and participation in society by other means (clubs, informal support) is not a trade-off or zero-sum game. It is plausible that people who are enabled to participate in society are more likely to find paid employment as well. When people have good and affordable public transport, good health and social care, and some money to spend, they are likely to go out and engage with others, rather than hide at home with the stigma of the allegedly 'useless'. And via these engagements with others they are more likely to have the opportunity to participate in meaningful communal work, learn of opportunities for paid work (for example in a cooperative), be referred by people who know and appreciate them, and so on. Equally important is that people who are outside the framework of a daily nine to five job keep up their work skills this way.

While we are convinced that a UBI would not mean that fewer people would want to work for money, there will be certain types of jobs that will probably no longer exist. These are the exploitative jobs that nobody wants to do *and* that are badly paid. These are jobs that are so stressful, dirty, difficult, dangerous or humiliating that people only do them because they have no choice. They are assembly line workers, toilet cleaners or workers in a slaughterhouse. These jobs are only done because people need an income. With a UBI, most people would still want to work, because few would happily live with an income just above the poverty line. But nobody would need to remain in exploitative, poorly paid work situations. As a result, the human work done at assembly lines, repetitive cleaning tasks and the mindless and soul-destroying work of telemarketing would likely be replaced by machines; in this sense, UBI would accelerate automation. Where human work cannot be replaced, people would need to get paid better, and have better working conditions, to keep doing it. The story of garbage collectors in New York is a case in point.

As the Dutch historian Rutger Bregman recounts, when several thousands of them went on strike in 1968 to protest their poor working conditions and low pay, the sanitary conditions of the city deteriorated so fast that the mayor gave in and the garbage collectors got their way (Bregman, 2016). Today, garbage collection is a much sought-after job in New York and in many other places of the world. The pay is considered fair, working times are reasonable, and instead of feeling humiliated because they are doing 'dirty work', garbage men and women are seen as part of the backbone of a city. In societies that introduce a UBI, at least some of the jobs that are badly paid, stressful and without prestige will follow the course of the garbage collectors. And if they do not, then, following the rationale of Rutger Bregman, perhaps they are not so important after all. Which brings us to the last part of our argument: the value of work.

According to Bregman, if you go on strike and nothing happens, then you have what the late London-based anthropologist David Graeber famously called a 'bullshit job' (Graeber, 2018) – a job that only exists to keep you busy. Our concern with the 'strike test' – the question whether or not other people will suffer if you do not show up for work – is that it creates 'false negatives'. False negatives are jobs that may fail the test because their value unfolds only later, and not in the moment it is done. Think of artists or nature conservationists and scientists. If these professions went on strike, their work may not be missed during the first days or weeks. Nobody would be immediately discomforted when a Latinist, a chef or a sculptor stopped working. But a society without classical scholars, artists or star-ranked chefs would be a culturally poorer place. What Bregman and Graeber get at is that societal prestige and remuneration is out of sync with what different professions contribute to society. The 'harsh truth is', Bregman says, 'that an increasing number of people do jobs that we can do just fine without. Were they to suddenly stop working, the world wouldn't get any poorer, uglier, or in any way worse'. Bregman names traders, corporate lawyers, and ad writers. 'Instead of *creating* wealth, these jobs mostly *shift* it around.' (Bregman, 2016, original emphasis) Some of them, we would add, not only do not create wealth, but they inflict harm; advertising or arms trading would fall into this category. Those speculating with financial products as well.

The COVID-19 crisis has not only shown the extent to which the relationship between the social value of work, its prestige and remuneration are disjointed, but also how normalised this mismatch has become. A good two years before the crisis, Barbara was the lead author on a paper suggesting that people's income should be more strongly related to the societal contribution that their profession makes (Prainsack and Buyx, 2018). What was at the time meant to be a provocative attempt to break into the hegemony of assuming that high pay means high value is now, we believe, of practical urgency. As many people have observed, we cannot go on clapping for 'key workers' without paying them fairly and improving their working conditions.

Universal basic income or job guarantee?

We want to conclude this chapter with a few words about an increasingly popular suggestion to address rising unemployment: a universal job guarantee. Similar to UBI, the economic crisis that was unleashed by the SARS-CoV-2 virus gave the job guarantee proposal an added urgency. Spearheaded by scholars in the Modern Monetary Theory (MMT) context, such as Pavlina Tcherneva and Stephanie Kelton, supporters of a job guarantee argue that a right to work for every person, and not 'money for nothing', is the right way to go. Every person who would like a job, these authors propose, whether full-time or part-time, and independent of their skills, should be given a job, paid from public funds, at a minimum hourly rate (in the United States, this would amount to $15 per hour, plus benefits). The money spent on these jobs, however, should not be seen as a subsidy for the unemployable, but as an investment in the real economy, as well as in sustainability. Local and communal job centres, instead of providing only job training and making people apply for jobs in the labour market, would curate and distribute a sufficient number of meaningful and suitable jobs to every applicant. These jobs would be under the banner of care: care for the environment (as part of Green New Deal proposals, see also Chapter 9), care for the community, and care for people (Tcherneva, 2018, 8).

We believe that job guarantees have a number of important advantages. First of all, they make us think differently about unemployment. Traditional economics frames unemployment as 'natural phenomenon'; a pool of jobless people just large enough to prevent rising inflation (Tcherneva, 2018, 3). (This has led to endless debates, and mathematical finessing, within economics about the optimal size of NAIRU. NAIRU is not an island in the Pacific but the acronym for 'non-accelerating inflationary rate of unemployment'. To each their own jargon.) Tcherneva distances herself from this dismal reasoning and conceives of unemployment as a public sector failure, created by misguided policies: 'the idea that some people will necessarily lose their jobs and livelihoods in the fight against other economic ills is a profound moral failure of the economics profession' (Tcherneva, 2018, 3). We also agree with Tcherneva and other proponents of job guarantee programmes that our societies are not short of work needing to be done: 'There is a lot of "invisible" environmental work that is labour intensive and can be done by people of various skill levels. This work must be performed on an ongoing basis and could provide the needed job opportunities, without competing with the private sector.' (Tcherneva, 2018, 17) Tcherneva and colleagues estimate the cost of a national job guarantee programme in the United States at about 1.5 per cent of GDP. At the same time, they argue, such a universal job guarantee would boost GDP, and any increases in price levels would be temporary, rather than causing enduring inflation (Prescod, 2020; Tcherneva, 2020).

While we wholeheartedly endorse most of the premises of the job guarantee proposal, we believe that a *universal* job guarantee is the wrong solution for the right problem. Like any good policy idea, its proof is in its realisation. That requires budgets, agencies, administrators, management, operating routines – the mundane stuff of policy implementation that is essential to the success of the programme. We foresee a number of problems here. First, it would be very bureaucratic and expensive in its administration. It would require a job to be found or created for every person who wants to work, regardless of where they live, of their particular limitations and strengths, skills and job preferences. In the first wave of the COVID-19 infection more than 30 million people in the US became unemployed within a matter of weeks. At the time of writing this book, over 10 million had found a job again, but it is hard to imagine that any administration can fashion millions of jobs on demand when they are needed most. Second, the programme consists of government officials working with ordinary people; public administration scholarship calls them street-level bureaucrats. Any student of street-level bureaucracy knows that this is difficult work with many imponderables. Most street-level bureaucrats are guided by professional values (Maynard-Moody and Musheno, 2003), but there is always the risk of inconsiderate, demeaning behaviour from the side of the official. This is particularly the case when the programme is contracted out to a private vendor, as the experiences in the UK with Universal Credit demonstrate. UBI on the other hand *reduces* bureaucracy. It consists of a computer program that transfers digital money from the government to people's current accounts and keeps track of their civic coordinates.

Third, it is likely that working age people who, against the backdrop of a job guarantee, would still choose not to work for money and would be stigmatised. Unless they are clearly too old or too ill, they would be branded as free riders, perhaps even to a greater extent than today. And we are not fully convinced that people working in a job created by a job guarantee programme would not be considered 'workfare scroungers' – as people having it easy, working in jobs tailor-made for their needs, with generous benefits. Fourth, the job guarantee programme conceives of work narrowly as paid employment. We are of course aware of the importance of work for people's identities. Work has many intangible rewards such as social contacts and friendships, giving structure to our day, creating a sense of achievement, or even pride in what we do and in what we are good at. But does this need to be restricted to paid work?

We believe that job guarantees are an ideal policy instrument if used in a targeted manner. For example, to support women seeking paid employment after having cared for children, or elderly workers who lost their jobs close to retirement age. But we believe that universal job guarantees are inferior to a UBI in preventing people from slipping into destitution. Despite the best intentions of their proponents, we fear that they may do more harm than good.

6

The return of good government

The poisoned chalice of government

Today, we as citizens of the advanced economies of the West inhabit a curious paradox. It is so familiar to us that we rarely give it a second thought. When we talk about our government, we usually do that in critical terms pointing out its failures and how politicians and bureaucrats cannot be trusted and make our lives difficult. At the same time, we enjoy the many services that the government provides, such as well-maintained roads, health care and education for all, income support for those who are less fortunate, legal protection against discrimination, and so on. On the one hand we are exposed to a steady stream of disparaging statements by economists, pundits and even elected officials about the intrinsic inefficiency of the state, its encroachment upon personal liberty and its constraining of the entrepreneurial spirit. In the United States any form of government intervention other than defence or policing is dismissed as 'socialism', often preceded by the adjective 'European style'. It is little wonder, then, that in survey after survey the public displays little affection for the officials and institutions of the state. This observation is borne out by reams of research in political science that demonstrates the public's profound distrust of politics and the institutions of government (Pew Research Center, 2019; see also EC, 2020). On the other hand, in every country a large constituency exists that values the collective provisions of the state, such as public health care, free education, accessible public transport, and public housing (Judt, 2010, 6). Even in socialism averse America a large majority of the public expresses support for health care that is free of the point of delivery, social security and a transition to a green society (Pew Research Center, 2020; KFF, 2020). Thus, while the public trusts the state in delivering large scale social provisions, it doubts its competence and has a hard time envisioning it as a force for the good.

This extended moral impasse about the proper place of government is not without consequences. For one thing, it has robbed us of a vocabulary for an impartial discussion of the proper tasks and achievements of government. In a domain so infected with reproach and denunciation, no statement about the state survives the sustained censure of its critics – particularly when it carries the authority of political and economic elites. When it comes to government, political invective has poisoned the very core of public reason. As some governments have badly stumbled in containing the COVID-19 pandemic and mitigating its fallout, this is a problem. Moreover, the pandemic is nested within an even bigger crisis: the looming climate catastrophe. Dealing urgently and adequately with the climate crisis requires levels of leadership, courage, wisdom, trust, and national and international policy coordination that dwarf everything that the pandemic requires of our governments. To put this differently, good, effective and just government, into which citizens can put their trust, is one of the most urgent challenges that humankind faces. In this chapter we will explain how in the first few decades after the Second World War we did reasonably well when it comes to good government, how we lost the way, and how we might regain it. This is a long and convoluted story that demonstrates, once again, the powerful laws of complexity at work. It is a combination of profound changes in the post-Second World War political economy, the emergence of economic doctrines that were increasingly hostile towards the state, and a revolution in administrative reform in the 1990s and beyond, that held, and still holds, governments of all political stripes in thrall.

The way we govern ourselves is a big topic not only in public debates but also within academic scholarship. The abundant literature in public administration (the discipline not the practice) focuses on public law, the organisation of government agencies, the role of administrators and the democratic legitimacy of administration. Lately it has also become sensitive to the role of discourse, the unquestioned collective understandings that shape administrative doctrine. Much of the literature has a reformist agenda; exhorting the reader how to do things better. Yet, despite the intellectual plenty of this literature, it displays three blind spots. First, it tends to draw the remit of public administration overly narrow as the design and delivery of social programmes and government services (such as obtaining a passport or maintaining parks). This makes sense insofar as for most people this is the face of government. But the COVID-19 crisis shows that governments have other vital responsibilities, such as maintaining a well-functioning public health system, supporting or doing basic scientific research, engage in effective economic policy, keep a sound national budget, maintain effective international relations, and draw in the expertise of a wide range of stakeholders in designing public policy.

Second, the public administration literature tends to portray administrative reform in rather monolithic, and often breathless, terms. Reform Z improves upon reform Y, which had already done away with the shortcomings of an earlier reform X. Each reform inexorably sweeps away the old rules, habits and organisations in its path. In reality, as we will see, new ideas have to be translated into new practices and organisations and, inevitably, under the influence of resistance, compromise and sensible adjustment, the new will be shaped by the old. This is the unavoidable implementation challenge that we encountered in the preceding chapters when we discussed the idea of universal job guarantees and the provision of affordable housing. The result is a bit like the accretion of the architectural styles of bygone ages in a medieval cathedral. Although this juxtaposition of administrative styles is an impediment to any easy reform, it is also a repository of good ideas and solutions of earlier times that can function as a lever for the imaginary reconstitution of public administration.

Finally, and perhaps most importantly, it is both impossible and unwise to detach changes in administrative doctrine and practice from questions of political economy and democracy. Hyperglobalisation (Rodrik, 2012), the concomitant rise of the giant transnational corporation (Crouch, 2011), the erosive influence on governments of both of these trends, the political weakening of social democracy, all had a pervasive influence on collective ideas of government – what government is, should be and can be. We will tell the larger story of globalisation, corporations and the finance sector in the next two chapters, but we want to flag here that it cannot be seen apart from the developments in the philosophy and practice of government. The result of these developments in the postwar political economy has been a profound reconfiguration of the relationship between the citizen and the state – both in the sense of how the state expects the citizen to think and behave and in the sense of what citizens expect from government and its institutions. This reconfiguration has been so deep and all-encompassing that it has attained hegemonic status. It would take a modern-day Foucault to write this genealogy of the loss of faith in government and the birth of a new, stripped-down, disempowered form of citizenship that is heavy on obligations and light on rights. This we cannot deliver, but we will try to sketch the contours of the story at least.[1]

This historical excursion is necessary for two reasons. First, although research in political science has shown, over and over again, that people distrust politicians and politics, not many people, certainly not outside the small specialist circle of public administration scholars, are aware of these historical developments that robbed them of effective, decent government. Ineffective, cynical, dishonest government is not a given, like the weather (although for human influences on the weather, see Chapter 9) but is, instead, a human construction. We will show, and that is our second point, that every twist and turn in the unhappy story of the decline in faith in government was the result of a deliberate decision of a cabal of business leaders, politicians and mercenary academics. In other words, there is nothing inevitable or law-like about the gradual descent into our current governmental dystopia. We do not need to be captives of a system of beliefs and practices that is antithetical to justice, decency and human flourishing. In a more positive vein: what was once undone can be constructed otherwise. In the final part of the chapter, we will present a historical example of good government and use it as a springboard for contemporary innovations in public administration.

The curious incapacitation of government

Ever since the revered German political philosopher Jürgen Habermas coined the term in the early 1970s, it is common among scholars of politics to think of the general loss of confidence in government institutions among the public as a legitimation crisis (Habermas, 1973). A legitimation crisis assumes a tacit contract between two parties: on one side the institutions that are constitutionally mandated to provide basic goods and services and secure the realm with a certain level of competence, efficacy and decency; on the other the public that gives or withholds its trust to them. It was another German scholar, the political economist Wolfgang Streeck, who pointed out that legitimacy in effect implies a three-way contract. The stability of the political-economic system requires that capital, its owners and managers, also needs to retain faith in government. With its own interests and desires, its own moods and creeds, its own strategies and intentions, the capital class is an actor in its own right in the vast realm of law, government and economy. And because it has something that any government needs, jobs and money, it might in effect be the most powerful partner in this three-way relationship. When capital loses faith in the government's ability to secure what it thinks of as an appropriate return on investment, it withholds and/or moves its resources. Streeck has taken this insight as the starting point for his breath-taking story of the development of what he calls 'postwar capitalism' to the current much-reviled neoliberalism (Streeck, 2017, 27). Between the lines it is the story of the limits of government in a progressively footloose and unbounded capitalist system.

'Postwar capitalism' was the outcome of the social pact between business and government after the Second World War had left most of Europe in ruins. Streeck is careful to argue that the 'postwar settlement' was not only a pragmatic agreement between labour and capital that enabled the reconstruction of the economy but also a new social philosophy, a new understanding of the social foundations of capitalism. It was the combined outcome of the experience of wartime solidarity and the moral bankruptcy of industrial and financial elites, many of whom had sympathised with fascism. In addition, in many European countries, communist parties who had stood up against Nazi oppression and sought just compensation for the working class who had fought in the war, scored large electoral victories. Against this background a broad societal coalition felt that the moral licence of capitalism as the best possible economic organisation was severely compromised and a renewal of its legitimation was inevitable. In terms of government, this meant a commitment of European governments to the public provision and management of housing, work, health, education, old age and protection against poverty. The result is the well-known welfare state with collective bargaining, mass education, affordable health care, stable public housing, post-tax income redistribution, and a basket of social protection programmes.[2]

What is often overlooked is that, in addition to an integrated set of social protection programmes, the welfare state also represented a new model of government. Large national agencies, populated by a cadre of well-trained and tenured administrators, capably 'produced' state-financed social protection, health and education services. For business, the settlement provided a stable investment climate, peaceful labour relations, strong investment in infrastructure and education, and a Keynesian macroeconomic policy that stimulated demand and kept interest rates low. Corporatist platforms, where representatives of labour, business and government regularly met, negotiated wages, managed labour relations and smoothed out potential conflicts of interest. Among administrators and politicians, developing the institutions of the welfare state led to a newfound confidence in their ability to govern effectively. Once the economy stood on its feet again, and backed by the tacit consent of the 'social partners', governments embarked on ambitious social engineering projects. In the 1960s the Dutch government, for example, introduced a generous Disability Law to compensate victims of workplace accidents (hailed at the time as the crown on the national social security building) and began comprehensive, nationwide school reform to fight entrenched inequality in the education system. These examples of assertive, sophisticated administrative behaviour are a far cry from the common understanding of government as an inefficient, wasteful deadweight on society – although, as we will see, administrative ambition did not exempt governments from the laws of complexity. At the end of the 1960s, just when, in most countries, welfare states (and in the United States, poverty reduction programmes) reached their apex, the postwar settlement began to unravel.

Streeck argues that business began to withdraw from the postwar settlement in response to the wave of strikes in 1968 and 1969. It feared increasing wage demands, a more self-conscious working class and ever rising expectations among the populace. In the United States the pending crisis revolved around identity and race; the Supreme Court's *Brown vs Board of Education* decision that stipulated desegregation of schools resulted in a furious reaction in conservative circles about the federal government's alleged assault on liberty (Maclean, 2017). Be that what it may, capital's second thoughts about the postwar settlement initiated a complex set of interlocking developments with dire consequences for the functioning of government.

Before long, the writing was literally on the wall. In 1973 Habermas published his *Legitimation Crisis* and James O'Connor his influential *The Fiscal Crisis of the State*. Ominously it was also the year of the oil crisis. Businesses began diverting labour and capital to low wage countries and pressure national governments for reform: deregulation, lower (corporate) taxes, less bureaucracy and in general a smaller state. With a state that had locked in expenditures and a citizenry that expected continued wage increases, something had to give. Governments reacted by printing money. Although it bought them social peace, with depressed economic growth, it plunged them into an inflationary spiral.

The end of the 1970s also inaugurated two grand narratives about government that left permanent marks on our collective image of government and governing. The first was the 'crisis of the welfare state' (OECD, 1981). A consensus emerged among economists, social scientists, conservative politicians and central bank governors that the integrated benefits and services that governments had created for its citizens had become unaffordable. In addition, and pre-echoing Reagan's infamous image of the 'welfare queen', the crisis narrative also cast suspicion on ordinary citizens. Overly generous social security arrangements, so the story went, had sapped them of industry and initiative. This part of the narrative prepared the population for the reforms and curtailment of social security programmes in the 1980s, and the individualisation of risk and benefits that came to characterise the relationship between citizens and the state.

With the economy in the doldrums and inflation running at 14 per cent in some countries, it was hard arguing against this reading of events. Moreover, there was some truth to the fact that idealistic interventionist governments had overreached and had fallen prey to the laws of complexity. For example, the eligibility criteria and replacement rate of the aforesaid Dutch Disability law were so generous that over time almost 900,000 workers (on a work force of five million) ended up drawing disability benefits. This was less the result of moral hazard on the part of wage earners as of the collaboration of employer's organisations and unions, who together administrated the programme, in misusing the Disability Law as a plush unemployment programme. In addition, welfare recipients were increasingly constructed as a suspect population whose eligibility and behaviour needed to be checked and monitored. As pointed out by political scientist Louise Haagh (2019), in 1980 fewer than a third of OECD countries performed systematic behavioural checks. By 2012, two thirds did so. This did not only change the lived experience of the state for welfare recipients, but it also affected the self-understanding of the state itself. It 'represents an extraordinary if silent transition in the role of the state from notionally a bulwark against market encroachment to arbitrator of civic expulsion' (Haagh, 2019, 26). By the start of the new millennium, the welfare state, and the governing model that supported it, had fallen more or less permanently into disrepute.

The second, ultimately more far-reaching, grand narrative of government failure is that of 'big government', a code word for an irrepressibly expansive, self-interested but intrinsically inefficient government. In the 1960s an economist from the University of Virginia, James Buchanan, published a series of books in which he presented an economics of government. 'Public choice economics', as the movement was innocuously called, created 'useful tools for analysing the incentive structures of public life' and 'nonmarket decision-making' (Maclean, 2017, 79, 85). One of the key insights of public choice was that just as in regular markets, in politics rationality and self-interest were closely linked. Political actors, such as politicians, voters, interest groups, and bureaucrats, were subject to the same self-interested, utility maximising behaviour as the buyers and sellers in the markets for fashion or consumer electronics. For example, the bureaucrat's utility was the size of his remit and agency, thus built into the very incentive structure of government was an intrinsic drive for expansion. Bureaucrats holds an information advantage over their political sponsors with regard to the 'goods' they produce with them. By controlling information, they are able to extract a surplus from their political superiors. Thus, government agencies produce a much larger output than is actually needed or required (Niskanen, 1971). This, according to public choice theorists, explained the expansion of government, both in monetary and organisational terms, in the 1960s and 1970s.

Clad in impressive looking mathematical formulas, public choice theory proved irresistible to a generation of scholars and politicians. Here, ostensibly, was the scientific proof of what many conservatives who held leading positions in business, academia and politics had suspected all along. Government had metastasised to the point that it stifled the market and ruined public finance. Public choice's main tenets – deregulation, privatisation, shrinking the state and stimulating the market – travelled across the Atlantic to influence Margaret Thatcher's offensive against the welfare state (MacNeal, 2017, 83). There was one small problem. Public choice had developed within a data-free environment and most of its hypotheses, when put to the test, proved to be empirically wrong. Bureaucrats were not always keen on expanding their agency when it meant taking tasks on board that did not fit their mission (Wilson, 1989). Salaries of bureau chiefs are not closely related to bureau size. Political controllers can rely on much more information than public choice theorists claim. It is impossible to say at what point agencies produce excessive output of public goods, just as it is difficult to determine the value of such goods (Self, 1993, 34). In fact, public choice theory was not a theory at all but a doctrine, an ideology, deliberately clad in the garments of science (Maclean, 2017, 80).

The aims of public choice doctrine were to protect property rights from the federal government, defend the freedom of corporations, and in general strip the state of all its functions except those of the libertarian night watchman state: defence against external and internal enemies, the upholding and adjudicating of property laws, and fending off threats to the optimal functioning of the free market (Gamble, 1994). In the words of historian Nancy Maclean: 'In the movement's view, government was the realm of coercion, and the market was the realm of freedom, of freely chosen, mutually valued exchange' (2017, 208). Public choice advocates sought to attain their ends by limiting taxation and shifting tax burdens to lower income groups, suppressing voting, restricting or even outlawing unions, deregulating corporations and financial institutions, curtailing social protection programmes and state-subsidised health care, privatising education and pensions, and changing the constitution to lock in these changes (Maclean, 2017, xvii). From the very start Buchanan's programme was financed by wealthy corporate backers, among which, over a period of 30 years, the billionaire industrialist Charles Koch was the main one. They provided the funds to establish a network of right-wing think thanks, such as the Cato Institute, the Heritage Institute, and the American Legislative Exchange Council. These organisations spread the public choice ideology and trained judges and public servants in its basic principles. This deliberate strategy to undermine the federal state and the democratic order was highly successful in the United States. It radicalised the Republican Party, reinvigorated a tradition of voter suppression, held back racial anti-discrimination laws, tilted the federal appeal courts and the Supreme Court to the right, and stripped away important state functions. It left the country disastrously unprepared for the COVID-19 pandemic. Perhaps its most important legacy is that it effectively undermined the idea that the state could – and should – be in the business of providing public goods. This is the background to the current moral impasse about government.

This is a very Anglophone story, and we will see that, despite the political-economic development from the postwar pact to unfettered globalised neoliberalism that affected most economies, capitalism took different forms in different parts of the world, creating different environments for government and public administration (Hall and Soskice, 2001). When we focus on government and public administration, to obtain a proper perspective on our current situation and the possibilities for change, we will have to discuss two more major public sector innovations. The first, New Public Management (NPM), although not as such anti-government, fitted the climate of distrust of the state. While many of its reforms were well-intended, it not only failed in many of its aims, but was also taken hostage in some countries by the public choice, small-state movement. The second, Interactive Government, emerged in continental Europe and was an attempt by governments to involve citizens in the formulation and implementation of public programmes. Taken together these trends and movements add up to a confusing patchwork of administrative approaches existing in parallel to each other. They also contain the seeds of progressive political and administrative reform.

At the end of the 1980s managerial approaches to public administration reform were in the air, but NPM burst upon the scene with the 1992 bestseller *Reinventing Government* by David Osborne and Ted Gaebler. The book's programmatic thrust can be inferred from its subtitle: *How the Entrepreneurial Spirit is Transforming the Public Sector*. On the surface the authors' recommendations are appealing enough. Reading from the Table of Contents we encounter 'Mission-Driven Government' (instead of rule-driven), Results-Oriented Government (instead of input-centred), as well as mottos such as 'Meeting the Needs of the Customer, not the Bureaucracy', and so on. With ten alluring visions these authors call for a government that, in the words of presidential candidate Al Gore 'works better and costs less'. What strikes the reader 30 years on is the evangelical fervour of the book. In the tradition of all evangelical tracts, its language is florid ('the bankruptcy of bureaucratic government', governments are in 'deep trouble' or even declared 'dead'), its black-and-white distinction between villains (inefficient bureaucracy) and heroes (entrepreneurial government) are stark, and its uplifting morality tales of failed programmes and miraculous healings by an 'innovative budget system' or the smart 'leveraging of resources' don't fail to inspire (Osborne and Gaebler, 1992). Lawd in heaven! Some programmes even turned a profit for the government!

NPM cut a wide swath through governments worldwide. Conservative and 'Third Way' Social-Democratic administrations provided a fertile ground for NPM. The famous 'Modernising Government' White Paper of the Blair government in the UK, with its emphasis on results-oriented governing, evidence-based policy and cutting unnecessary regulation, is just one famous example from the NPM playbook (Cabinet Office, 1999). In practice NPM not only failed to deliver on its promises but also facilitated a number of particularly destructive policies such as privatising public services and ruthless cost cutting to bring down the budget deficit.

The British public administration scholar Christopher Hood has done us a great favour by summarising the main components of NPM and, 25 years later, evaluating its outcomes (Hood, 1991; Hood and Dixon, 2015). NPM, according to Hood, rests on seven principles: hands-on professional management, explicit standards of performance, to be used as an instrument of output control, disaggregation of administrative units to be financed and managed on a contract basis, competition, introduction of 'proven' corporate management techniques, and cost cutting (Hood, 1991, 5). In NPM citizens were primarily 'customers' of public administration, not people with rights. NPM presented itself as a value-neutral, 'portable' solution to a more effective and efficient government.

It is to the credit of Hood, and his collaborator Ruth Dixon, that they engaged in one of the few dispassionate evaluations of NPM. They restricted themselves to the UK but there is no reason to believe that the situation is different in other countries. Their verdict leaves nothing to the imagination: '[O]ver a thirty-year period of successive reforms, one of the most commented-on government systems in the world [the United Kingdom] exhibited a striking increase in running or administration costs in real terms, while levels of complaint and legal challenge also soared.' (Hood and Dixon, 2015, 1) Doing less for more, while disenfranchising the citizen. The authors see no evidence of improved quality of services, and neither did the more corporate-style management and the introduction of digital technologies bring down personnel or running costs (Hood and Dixon, 2015, 186).

Hood and Dixon take great care to cut through the rhetoric to back their conclusions up with sophisticated reasoning and assiduously collected, carefully arranged numbers. Perhaps they are too careful. A group of scholars at the University of Manchester applied forensic accounting to one of the most popular elements of NPM: outsourcing public services to private vendors (Bowman et al, 2015). What they find is a pattern of value extraction and rentierism (Christophers, 2020) in which private industry and government are equally complicit. They observe 'unjustifiable profit taking in sheltered activities when limited capital investment is required', 'Cost reductions that improve margins … by eroding wages and conditions which can undermine quality services'. They observe a pattern of 'designed fiascos' (such as disciplining welfare claimants or incarcerating asylum seekers, where the outsourcing firm takes the blame instead of the government, followed by a ritualised Select Committee inquiry) and 'routine cockups' where the outsourcing company, often with 'limited sectoral expertise' dramatically fails to deliver (such as with the privatisation of probation services in the UK, or recently the SARS-CoV-2 infecton track and trace system). The Manchester researchers also observed that the practice of outsourcing has created giant international conglomerates, or rather networks of firms headed by an equity company established in a tax shelter, that use acquisitions and internal loans to artificially inflate losses and avoid corporate taxes. They call these practices '[exposing] essential service delivery to financialised practices' (Bowman et al, 2015, 10–13). The result is the transfer of large amounts of taxpayer money to the shareholders of the outsourcing conglomerates.

Public administration in the age of privatised Keynesianism

What explains the worldwide success of NPM? To answer this question, we need to return to the development of the political economy after the crisis of the welfare state. Streeck argues that after the spike in inflation in the late 1970s, national governments had to find other ways to pacify social conflict and meet citizen expectations regarding service delivery and middle class lifestyle. They first resorted to borrowing on international capital markets to make up for the budgetary shortfall that was the result of lower corporate taxes (often as a result of the misguided macroeconomic policy that lower corporate taxes would be compensated for in higher economic output and tax returns). At the end of the 1980s international rating agencies began to judge national debt levels of the advanced economies as dangerously high. Moreover, the 1992 Maastricht treaty bound every EU country to a cap on budget deficits and national debt. As a result, states resorted to a third strategy to expand the stock of financial resources in the political economy available for redistribution. They banked, literally, on the deregulation of the financial sector to stimulate and facilitate private debt to finance public services and purchasing power. Through generous tax deductions and co-financing, citizens took on private debt to finance housing, education, health care and pensions. This 'privatised Keynesianism' was a boon to the financial industry and contributed to its rapid global expansion. It also cemented the understanding of the citizen as someone who was responsible for their own labour market qualification and service consumption.

Some of the precepts of NPM have no doubt improved efficiency and service delivery. For example, many government agencies have become customer oriented. The digitisation of government processes, although accompanied by spectacular and expensive software development failures, has also improved customer experience. When applied to the more logistical aspects of public service delivery – issuing passports or drivers licences, maintaining parks – corporate production examples may enhance efficiency. But NPM was pushed into sensitive areas such as prison management, care for the elderly or even army tasks, where accountability was low, and the rights of vulnerable groups were sacrificed on the altar of shareholder value. NPM's repertoire of techniques – performance indicators, outsourcing, performance-related pay, auditing, consumer boards – has changed the face of public service delivery in many countries. A vocabulary of 'customers' and 'managers' has supplanted that of 'citizens' and 'civil servants'. NPM was the perfect ideology to enable the responsibilisation of citizens and the financialisation of government services. In practice, the most popular elements of NPM were cost cutting (particularly after the enormous increase in national debt after the financial crisis of 2008), the outsourcing of public services to private companies, the rise of the manager (often with salaries that mirrored those in the private sector) and the creation of dedicated units for message control.

In addition to NPM, in the same period many governments began to experiment with participatory forms of government, particularly, but not exclusively, in the continental democracies of Europe. Under labels such as 'interactive governance' (Edelenbos and van Meerkerk, 2016) or 'government-driven democratisation' (Warren, 2014) governments began to involve citizens and societal organisations in the design and implementation of policy. While NPM, at least in its real-world incarnation, often results in the disempowerment of citizens, the aim of interactive governance is to enrich democracy, to expand the scope, franchise and authenticity of democratic process (Dryzek, 1996). Governments were drawn to civic participation through a combination of push and pull factors. To many local governments for example it had become clear that they had lost the trust of citizens. In other instances, the decentred policy system contained so many veto points that only close collaboration between stakeholders made effective decision making possible. In general, interactive governance is more frequently encountered at local than national levels. Interactive governance usually takes two forms: top down, government-driven; and bottom up, citizen-driven. Both encounter serious implementation problems in practice. Many administrators are unwilling or unable to give up what they see as their mandated right to collective decision making. While they welcome increased interaction with citizens or citizen initiatives, in the final analysis political expediency or administrative routine prevails. Citizen initiatives to provide public goods and services (civic enterprises or commons; see Wagenaar and Healey, 2015) are applauded and sometimes subsidised by politicians and administrators but are often frustrated by dense regulation in their specific domain of activity (Wagenaar, 2019).

To illustrate the complexity of administrative reform, in many countries NPM and interactive governance, despite their different rationales and effects, exist alongside each other, with classical hierarchical public administration in the background to regulate the behaviour of privatised and civic organisations. Public administration has in effect entered a state of continuous, unceasing innovation. The Netherlands, for example, was an early, enthusiastic adopter of NPM-type administrative innovation. In areas such as health care, social and youth services, and housing it implemented large scale privatisation and competition. Housing associations and railways were privatised, energy provision was sold to large international agglomerates, health care was uncoupled from the state and its financing and management assigned to an oligopoly of large insurance firms. All these interventions were accompanied by serious budget cuts. But both railways and health insurance are strictly regulated by the state and monitored by parliament. At the same time social services now had to compete for contracts, resulting in shortages and discrepancies between the need for and the supply of services.

The reform of social care in the Netherlands is a good example of the complexities of contemporary public administration created by the addiction to administrative reform. With a rapidly growing social care budget consuming 10 per cent of the national budget (CBS, 2020), the government decided for an overhaul of the social care system. It was to be devolved to local governments (NPM) and involve civic and religious organisations, as well as families, in the provision of social care to the sick and elderly (interactive governance). It is typical of the times that the reform balanced three incompatible goals: less government (NPM), more individual responsibility, and a 'caring society' (Jager-Vreugdenhil, 2012, 21). With the devolution came a 25 per cent reduction of the available budget as part of Dutch austerity politics (NPM). Local governments overwhelmed by their new responsibilities often contracted care out to for-profit care companies (NPM). In most cases this meant that care workers were laid off and rehired at lower wages and more precarious work conditions. At the same time citizen cooperatives sprung up to plug gaps in the provision of care (interactive governance). However, many of these cooperatives were frustrated by regulation (hierarchical government) and ran into conflicts with professional service providers who felt threatened by the citizens. In most municipalities, citizens now have to navigate a constantly changing maze of private and public providers to obtain necessary care.

What are the prospects for successful administrative reform?

What are we to make from this tangled history of post-Second World War public administration? First, as we have seen, for an adequate comprehension of the complexities of administrative trends we cannot consider them in isolation from their political-economic context. Our understanding of the limits and possibilities of public administration and the reach of democratic rule are shaped by the deep organisation of economic life. For example, we are currently living in what Streeck calls a debt state (see also Graeber, 2011). Streeck defines it narrowly as the state's increasing dependence on credit for its financial needs (2017, 72). But after the 2008 financial crisis everyone is indebted. Although for different reasons and with different consequences. A decade-long, ultra-low interest rate environment has spurred corporations to become highly leveraged. The withdrawal of public funding has compelled some public organisations such as universities to borrow large sums of money to invest in campus improvements. The steady decline of wages and the rise of insecure, non-guaranteed labour has forced people to take on high levels of debt, through credit cards, payday loans and subprime credit, to make ends meet.

The result is that the fate of citizens, businesses and state governments has become deeply entangled with the international financial sector. In Chapter 1 we described what this means for citizens: a growing number of people discover that they have lost all the means for an ordinary middle class existence and become nomads, literally and metaphorically (moving through flats, jobs, whenever and wherever they are available). A much larger number precariously hangs on, unable to satisfy even the most basic needs and have to rely on food banks or friends. The notion of 'deaths of despair' (2020) coined by economists Ann Case and Angus Deaton refers to the consequences of this precarity epidemic for the physical and mental health of entire societies: while deaths from smoking and other problems are decreasing, the new killers are opioids, alcohol and suicide. Many people feel they have nothing to live for.

States cannot escape the demands of bondholders and banks either. To secure the servicing of debt obligations the latter will try to influence the goals and activities of the state. In this they usually find a willing partner as states use their debt overhang to rationalise ongoing cuts in public services. Even in the best of circumstances capitalism is an uneasy alliance between social justice and market recompense.[3] The latter is the expectation of just rewards for successful entrepreneurial performance and is regarded a necessary condition for the adequate functioning of the market. Social justice is a more complex construct based on collective ideas about fairness, solidarity, and human rights (Streeck, 2017, 58). The relationship between the two is highly asymmetrical, with social justice seen as intruding upon 'self-evident' market recompense. (Public choice was entirely based on the unquestioned, obvious nature of market recompense.) States have to find a compromise between justice and recompense. Over the past three decades the balance between the two has decidedly shifted in favour of the latter. The postwar settlement, and the welfare state that followed from it, were successful examples of such a compromise. But as we have seen, the business sector withdrew from the pact and in the hyperglobalised, neoliberal economic climate, states increasingly sided with business and finance, and were willing to impose standards, regulations and tax arrangements that favour global trade on domestic institutions (Rodrik, 2012, 222). The COVID-19 crisis has shown that this trend has reached the point that the capitalist order can no longer reproduce itself.

Second, as we have seen, in most countries there is not one, coherent, administrative regime in place. Administrative reform is oversold. Despite the overheated rhetoric of public innovation, the business of government is a pragmatic answer to a nation's particular challenges, configuration of values and historical legacy. Most public innovation quickly runs into the reality of its implementation. This makes public innovation 'precarious', as Wagenaar and Wood argue (2018). They mean that innovation in the public sector is less a succession of exalted schemes than a pragmatic reaction to changing circumstances; 'less 'intentional development' and more practical, pragmatic, and usually local, problem solving.' (Wagenaar and Wood, 2018, 157). In this dance of resistance and accommodation, 'one actor's innovation is another actor's invitation to move into a field and neutralise a threat to one's dignity, freedom, cherished life, work routines, moral worth or community cohesion' (Wagenaar and Wood, 2018, 157).

Inevitably, administrative reform implies institutional reform, and changing institutions, as every political scientist will tell you, is a tall order. Political institutions form the legal and regulatory skeleton of society and are therefore seen as permanent, stable and resilient. Institutions are the anchors with which the ferment of social and political life is moored. They are not supposed to be changed easily. The American political scientist Christopher Ansell thinks that this normative understanding of institutions has made us guilty of enshrining them. More contemporary understandings of political institutions think of institutions as cultural artefacts that 'sustain and accumulate meaning', a form of soft technology meant to address and solve collective problems (Ansell, 2011). 'To abstract a social object from these practices, values and loyalties is to commit an error of reification', Ansell (2011, 37) says. He encourages us to think about institutions 'transactionally as dynamic, ongoing interactions between concepts, experience, and situations' (Ansell, 2011, 39). Surveying this confusing landscape, Wagenaar and Wood (2018, 158) argue for a process of guided administrative change that is democratically embedded, distributed, and pragmatic, a form of institutional-design-in-practice as an open and inclusive conversation between societal challenges, collective ideals and institutional forms (Wagenaar and Wenninger, 2020, 416).

How realistic is such a process of collective institutional design-in-practice? With global markets stacked up against sovereign nations, governments in many countries in disrepute over their handling of the coronavirus crisis and the earlier 2008 financial meltdown, and a public that is not only distrustful of the state but in some cases openly hostile towards democratic institutions, how likely is it that a fragile process of dispersed institutional design will ever succeed? Our answer is that we can do worse than find inspiration in historical examples. In an article about 'Red Vienna', that remarkable episode in enlightened public administration in Vienna between 1919 and 1933, we showed what a determined administration can achieve (Wagenaar and Wenninger, 2020). Facing the economic, infrastructural, and human devastation of the First World War on its installation, in the space of a mere 14 years, the new Social-Democratic city administration designed and implemented an integrated housing, public health, education, health and cultural policy that has withstood the test of time. As we have seen in Chapter 4, more than a century later, Vienna is a still an acknowledged exemplar of a fair, just and equitable approach to affordable housing. The elements of this remarkable success were a body of well-trained civil servants who were endowed with a clear administrative ethos, creative and progressive tax policies, a pragmatic approach towards experimentation, the institutionalisation of solutions that worked, and a progressive humanist vision of improving the physical, mental and educational condition of the working class. The government of Red Vienna returned values of fairness, justice, equality and aesthetics to government.

Inspiring as the example of Red Vienna may be, to a contemporary public its story is at best incomplete. To the administrators of Red Vienna their model and ideal was classical Weberian public administration, which they employed creatively and pragmatically. Their knack for integrated government, based on administrative expertise and a clearly articulated public ethos, can still instruct us about the possibilities of the hierarchical state. But for one thing, the politicians and administrators of Vienna's Social-Democratic administration did not contemplate civil society participation. While they were masters of political mobilisation, promoting dozens of workers', women's or voters' organisations to create popular support for their policies, the participation of civil society organisations or citizens in the process of government was simply not on their radar. This does not fly today. Whatever their flaws and limitations, interactive government, governance-driven democratisation, citizen engagement and co-production have become commonplace in today's repertoire of governance techniques. Moreover, in those cases where governments have steadfastly ignored society's needs or values, grassroots movements emerge that articulate the issue at hand and challenge authorities to take appropriate action. Some of the most vital issues of our times, such as racial injustice, gun control, climate change, sexual harassment and child poverty, have been confronted by grassroots movements. These extra-parliamentary movements have mobilised effective opposition, influenced the political agenda and generated new ideas. Given the resistance of corporate and financial institutions, the weakness of our beleaguered governments and the fragility of our democratic institutions, we need these grassroots movements to articulate an agenda for change, feed us with knowledge of the state we are in, and keep up the pressure to make that change happen.

Modern administrations like to present themselves as open to learning. In fact, throughout history governments have copied and adapted innovations that worked elsewhere. That is how the welfare state developed from its late 19th century Bismarckian origins, for example. But nowadays government learning is biased towards corporations, financial institutions and neoliberal doctrine. While every self-respecting national and local administration sports a 'behavioural insights' (aka 'nudging') unit, collaborating with citizen cooperatives or grassroots movements is decidedly less popular. But vigorous participatory policy making is how institutional design-in-practice in practice would look like. For one thing it would revive the generative power of big ideals (instead of nudging people to adopt practices that fit middle class ideals of rational behaviour). Big organising, as Monbiot (2017, 168) calls it; policies commensurate with the scale of the challenge we face, pursuing big targets and the mobilisation of volunteers. Red Vienna taught us that ambituous utopian ideals serve to guide transformational change. In other words, civic engagement and public administration can, and should, work in tandem, expediting collective problem solving and enriching democratic process. As we will show in the final two chapters, the road to effective cooperation between citizens and institutionalised government is strewn with obstacles. But grassroots movements and civic engagement show us a new way of participatory politics.

By now we have strayed into the terrain of democratic reform. That is an important discussion to have but we will postpone it until our concluding chapter. Also, reform is not restricted to administrative reform. Important as it is, in the final analysis it is a topic for specialists. The imaginative reimagination of other societal domains is what awaits us. We need urgent reforms in corporate responsibility, global finance and climate change. And fortunately, we do not need to execute some form of triage on these huge issues, and devote our energies to, for example, fighting the impending climate catastrophe while we put public sector reform on the back burner. History has taught is that public administration is by its nature reactive. Just as the welfare state forged new practices of public administration, so will successfully dealing with these three challenges. Thus, it is now that we turn to corporate responsibility, global finance and the climate challenge.

Real corporate responsibility

Moving factories

On 3 October 2007, writes the British journalist James Meek, the 500 workers at the Cadbury chocolate factory in the town of Keynsham were told that their jobs would be moved to Poland. 'Highly paid, permanent, solidly pensioned jobs', he adds. It does not surprise the reader that the move was exclusively motivated by the circumstance that 'their Polish replacements could do the same job for less than one fifth of the money', and not because Cadbury's products were not selling, or because the factory was unprofitable (Meek, 2017). On the day of the announcement the managers locked the workers out and posted security guards at the factory gate. They feared a violent reaction. But the workers, many of whom had worked at the company for decades, ruefully remarked that management had misjudged the mood in the community and that the residents would have done anything to keep the factory in Keynsham.

Meek's article about the move of the Cadbury factory to the Polish region of Skarbimierz encapsulates everything that is problematic about the corporate sector today. He describes in detail how the history of the company was joined up with the culture and history of the town. Generations of Keynsham residents had been employed by the company. The town's economic destiny, its collective pride and its residents' identity were tied up with the Cadbury plant. The company had profited from the availability of public infrastructure, the skills and education of its workforce, the invisible labour of women, the natural resources it used, and the state's investment in research and innovation. Similar to companies all over the world, Cadbury owed a debt to the society, community and natural environment that made it possible for the company to operate.

In the end all this did not weigh in when the corporation decided to move its production technology to Poland. Helped by generous tax breaks and subsidies from both the Polish government and the EU, and a local workforce that was willing to work for less than the workers in Keynsham, Cadbury's managers moved the entire plant. It must be added that Cadbury's Board had been under fierce pressure from its major shareholders, in particular a hedge fund that was financed by a Qatar sovereign wealth fund, to increase return on capital.

Corporate social responsibility

People who do not live in Keynsham will probably shrug their shoulders when they read the story of Cadbury's move to Poland. Firms that bring their production line to low wage countries are a common feature of modern capitalism. The economic rationale has the force of the inevitable. Companies need to do what is best for them, right? Yet, in the business literature, a rich body of work exists on *corporate social responsibility* (CSR). It is based on the idea that entrepreneurs and managers do not only have a responsibility to shareholders but also to stakeholders (Spreckley, 1981). The British political economist Colin Crouch describes CSR in economic terms as 'behaviour by firms that voluntarily takes account of the externalities produced by their market behaviour' (2011, 138). 'Externalities' is economese for the costs of business transactions that are not factored into the price of the product. Classic examples are air or surface water pollution that occur in the course of the production process. A contemporary example would be the loss of privacy as the cost of using the internet.

CSR gained currency in the 1970s and obtained additional momentum in the 1980s and 1990s, when global players such as Nestlé and Nike faced mounting criticism following their involvement in the baby milk scandal and their exploitation of child labour respectively. Robert Braun, a social theorist at the Institute for Advanced Studies in Vienna, defines CSR as the 'integration of the stakeholders' values and interests into the corporation's business operation' (2019, 18). Braun is interested in introducing democracy inside the corporation. Not the older socialist workers' democracy, but a broader stakeholder democracy that is fit for our pluralist times, where stakeholders become 'citizens of the corporation' and rules and institutions of 'deliberative stakeholder democracy' are set up within businesses (Braun, 2019, 6). CSR's growing popularity within the business domain, however, is also linked to the idea that profits can be increased when a company displays its socially responsible and 'ethical' awareness (see also McGoey, 2015). There is a sizeable literature assessing the extent to which the embrace of CSR improves market performance (for example, van Beurden and Gössling, 2008). Doing good should not mean that one should lose money.

In the age of shareholder primacy people might be surprised to learn that the responsibilities of the business corporation have been vigorously debated since at least the 1930s. In the late 19th century the privately held company made way for the 'public' corporation. 'Public', here, must be understood in two senses. First, these new business entities were legal constructions made possible by the laws and institutions of the state (in some places, businesses received time-limited charters from the state; when the charter expired without being renewed, this meant the end of the business). Second, companies issued shares into the public domain. These were held by thousands of individual or institutional investors. The American corporate law scholar Lynn Stout argues that this led to a 'qualitative change' in the way people understood the relationship between private property and the business corporation. Who owned the corporation? Who made it possible? On the one hand were scholars who argued that the shareholders were the owners of the company and that it was the task of management to maximise the value of their shares. On the other side were scholars who emphasised the public aspect of the modern corporation and therefore ascribed a much broader charter to it. Investors were believed to form a cross section of middle class society, who have roots in the community and care about its welfare. In addition to making a profit, the business corporation is therefore responsible for the wellbeing of society at large, including the employees and customers of the corporation (Stout, 2012, 17).

By the early 1950s the argument was decided in favour of those who held a broader view of the purpose of the business corporation. Managers held corporate powers 'in trust for the entire community' (Stout, 2012, 17). Since then, more or less elaborate doctrines of CSR have been formulated. An important one is the 'triple bottom line'. It not only admonishes firms to pay attention to ecological and societal value creation in addition to economic goals, but also develops a kind of accounting procedure for assessing the extent that businesses have reached these goals. Other authors have contributed to CSR doctrine by articulating the concept of stakeholder. Braun quotes Edward Freeman who has extended the notion of stakeholder from stockholder to everyone who has a stake in or a claim on the firm. These include suppliers, customers, employees, stockholders and the local community. Freeman maintains that managers bear a 'fiduciary relationship' to these diverse stakeholders (Braun, 2019, 57). Freeman formulated his stakeholder doctrine before environmental concerns began to dominate the agenda. The environmental economist Kate Raworth has extended CSR to the age of climate change. In her view businesses have five options in their relationship to the natural environment: do nothing, do what pays (introduce ecological measures because it is more efficient), do your fair share (for example channel some of your investments into green energy, a well-known strategy of the fossil industry), do no harm (design, produce and distribute your products such that they have zero environmental impact), and be generous. That last response requires a transition from an extractive to a regenerative or circular design of the strategic and operational routines of the business (Raworth, 2017, Chapter 6).

These are lofty words but, apparently, they fell on deaf ears with the management of Cadbury. The managers did not show much awareness that they felt responsibility for the wellbeing of the town and its citizens/employees. The term 'fiduciary' implies trust and it is here that the reality of CSR clashes with the ideal. Meek does not report that Cadbury was criticised by the British government or the unions for not living up to the ideals of CSR. Quite the opposite as we said before. Closing your production line and moving it abroad is expected behaviour. It is part of the collateral damage of modern capitalism. The question should be therefore: what causes the discrepancy between the ideal and reality of CSR?

On 24 April 2011 the Rana Plaza building on the outskirts of Dhaka, the capital of Bangladesh, collapsed, killing 1,125 people and injuring 2,000. The building housed a garment factory with over 3,000 workers and their machines. The disaster threw a light on the exploitative practices that governed the supply chains of the western fashion industry. Sanchita Banerjee Saxena, executive director of the Institute of South Asia Studies at the University of Berkeley, is one of the leading authorities on the South-East Asian garment industry. She describes the aftermath of the disaster. Western fashion brands and companies, such as H&M, Ralph Lauren and Gap, under pressure from the outrage about the loss of life of workers working under hazardous conditions for low wages, created two organisations to monitor the local factories. The first is the *Accord in Fire and Building Safety in Bangladesh*. It is an agreement between global unions, over 180 retailers, and brands from over 20 countries on four continents. The Accord is legally binding. The second is the *Alliance for Bangladesh Worker Safety* that covers 28, mainly US, companies. With these accords the companies involved set up so-called 'surrogates', third parties that are invested with the legal authority to monitor the situation in the garment factories. These international agreements have been hailed as examples of CSR at its best and even a new form of global governance driven by the private sector (Saxena, 2018). Yet, Saxena is less sanguine about their outcomes.

Saxena shows that the agreements governing the garment industry put the responsibility for the improvement of the conditions exclusively with the local contractors. This leaves the larger supply-chain outside of the monitoring regime. But, as Saxena shows, the local contractors still face 'extreme pressure' from western brands to deliver at the lowest cost in the shortest time frame. This leads to a lot of subcontracting, where workplace conditions are as bad as ever, and that is not covered by the monitoring regime. In practice, the monitoring regime becomes a 'tick the boxes' exercise that has symbolic value for the websites of the brands but ignores the deeper problems in the factories that are related to health, wellbeing, skills training, gender discrimination and sexual violence. Finally, the accords ignore the many civil society organisations within Bangladesh that strive to better the position of the, largely female, workforce in the factories. Saxena concludes that we need to involve these local stakeholders in improving the situation for those in the community who are at the bottom of the garment industry's value chain.

We can draw two important lessons from this example. Even with the best of intentions and in the best of circumstances CSR solutions are not exempt from the implementation gap – the difference between policy on paper and policy in action. In that respect they are like every other policy intervention. But as Saxena makes clear, the international agreement did not lift the pressure on local factory owners that issues from the business model of the western brands. And that business model is governed by the doctrine of shareholder value maximisation. To understand how the shareholder value doctrine came to be standard practice within the business world and clouded the prospects for businesses to take their responsibility for the community and the environment seriously, we need to add more elements to the story of the emergence of our postwar political economy.

Shareholder value and the rise of the giant transnational corporation ...

Arguably the most influential of the publications on CSR was also the one that more or less killed the idea. In 1970, the Chicago School, free market economist Milton Friedman published an article in the *New York Times Magazine* in which he argued that the managers of a business corporation only had one responsibility: to increase its profits and thereby the wealth of its shareholders. What is remarkable about Friedman's position is not its return to an argument about corporate purpose that had already been made in the 1930s, but the speed with which it came to dominate the world of business, law, government, economics and corporate practice. By the start of the new millennium the 'Friedman doctrine' as it came to be called was hegemonic. As Stout (2012, 21) writes:

> [B]y the close of the millennium ... [m]ost scholars, regulators and business leaders accepted without question that shareholder wealth maximization was the only proper goal of corporate governance. Shareholder primacy had become dogma, a belief system that was rarely questioned, seldom explicitly justified, and had become so pervasive that many of its followers could not even recall where or how they had first learned of it.

How could one article in the *New York Times* have such a wide impact? How had the world changed so that it was ready for Friedman's extremist standpoint?

Since the early 1970s the world economic order has undergone a series of complex, discordant changes in the domains of law, regulation, technology, transportation, business practices and economic discourse. These changes can be summarised with the term 'hyperglobalisation'. Few people would contest the benefits of international trade. It enables a UK family to enjoy French wine and Italian prosciutto. It allows Chinese students to enrol in British and American universities, and young Australians to work in South Korea or Taiwan. In the 17th century the trade in grain from the Baltic states and wine and oil from Portugal brought unprecedented wealth to the sea faring Low Lands (the Netherlands, in today's language). International trade has brought prosperity to countless millions in developed and developing nations.

Hyperglobalisation is of a different order. It is what brings £3 T-shirts and £15 dresses to large clothing chains such as Primark and Zara. It allows Dutch fisherman to catch shrimp in the North Sea, which are then transported to Morocco to be peeled there by local women and transported back to be sold in Dutch supermarkets. It makes possible the creation of complex supply chains in the automotive industry to set up shop in low wage countries to bring down labour costs. It puts strawberries and avocados on our breakfast table during the winter months. Hyperglobalisation is the process of designing national and international institutions and regulations in such a way that they enable unfettered international trade. It means the adulation of a country's 'international competitiveness' by economists and politicians. As we will see in the next chapter, it also means giving free rein to financial institutions, with decidedly negative outcomes. In practice, this type of globalisation means that domestic interests and national democracy have to bow to international trade and finance. As the Harvard trade economist Dani Rodrik summarises: 'Globalisation became an imperative, apparently requiring all nations to pursue a common strategy of low corporate taxation, tight fiscal policy, deregulation, and reduction of the power of unions.' (2012, 76) For many people hyperglobalisation symbolises the exploitation by multinational corporations of labourers, farmers, developing nations and the environment (Rodrik, 2012, xiii).

At the heart of hyperglobalisation is the 'giant transnational firm'. Colin Crouch defines it according to two criteria: it dominates its particular slice of the market; and it is active across more than one national jurisdiction (Crouch, 2011, 49). Think of Exxon, Google, Unilever or Volkswagen, which are active in dozens of countries all over the world and have annual budgets that dwarf those of many countries. Entry barriers and changes in antitrust law, fuelled by the economic doctrine of shareholder value, have allowed such vast concentrations of corporate power that markets have de facto dissolved in certain areas of economic activity. These corporate powerhouses wield their might by engaging in the simultaneous takeover of the market *and* of national governments. Businesses – the carbon industry, pharmaceutical companies, food and tobacco, car makers, the finance industry – each year spend hundreds of millions on lobbying and engaging in co-regulation with public authorities, writing the very regulation that is supposed to constrain their activities. The distinction between private economic entities and governments has been blurred to the point that they form a symbiotic relationship. The transnational firm has become a powerful political actor in its own right, making both the idea of the 'market' and of democracy more or less meaningless. This is a strong claim that requires further explanation.

In the preceding chapter we discussed how the public choice doctrine shaped a particular dystopian understanding of government. We showed how public choice translated into new administrative practices, foremost among them the downsizing of government by cutting budgets and contracting out public services to private companies. What we did not mention was that public choice had a legal counterpart in the influential 'Law and Economics' movement, spearheaded by the enterprising law professor Henry Manne. Law and Economics sought to provide a legal basis for 'unregulated corporate capitalism' and liberating corporations from the 'distortions … of government intervention' (Maclean, 2017, 185). It sought 'to make the protection and enhancement of corporate

profits and private wealth the cornerstones of (the) legal system'
(Mclean, 2017, 126). The Law and Economics doctrine was the legal
expression of the buccaneering, free market, Chicago School brand of
economics. Similar to Buchanan's public choice movement in public
administration, Manne's crusade was lavishly bankrolled by the dark
money of wealthy industrialists. In its summer schools and seminars, it
indoctrinated hundreds of legal scholars and future judges. According to
some commentators, the Law and Economics movement amounted to
a hugely successful conservative revolution in American law (Maclean,
2017, 126; Stout, 2012, 19). Taken together, the public choice and
Law and Economics doctrines profoundly influenced how we think
about the nature of the market, the role of law in regulating business,
the face of business and the place of corporations in the public sphere.
This is important for our understanding of the responsibility we assign
to firms for sustainability and social welfare – differently put, for how
we understand CSR.

As every introductory course in economics teaches, the idea of a
self-regulating market requires a large number of actors (firms and
customers) and full information (on product performance, features,
quality, availability of service, and so on) to make it possible for the
customer to interpret prices as a reliable indicator of value. Thus,
if I am interested in, let us say, buying a bicycle, I have a choice
between a simple bike to get around in the city or a swanky racing
bike with a high-end gear system and a lightweight carbon frame.
The latter will set me back several thousand pounds, but (assuming
I can afford it) I know that I was free to make a choice that accords
with my needs. The public choice/Law and Economics doctrines
changed all that.

For almost a century the market was regulated by antitrust law. In
case one or a few firms began to dominate the market, antitrust law
could force either a break-up of the firm or the entry of other firms.
The purpose of the laws was to protect consumer choice. Crouch
explains that antitrust law protected citizens not just from overly large
concentrations of business power but also of political power. 'To the
extent that economic power could be a major source of political power
too, antitrust policy protected democratic pluralism as much as it did
market competition' (Crouch, 2011, 54). The aversion of the public
choice ideologues towards the state was such that they looked for ways
to bypass the state altogether in cases of market distortion. The solution
was to discard the idea of consumer choice and replace it with that
of consumer welfare (Crouch, 2011, 55). Consumer welfare is not
about maximising customer choice but about securing the *conditions*

for choice. And, so the reasoning goes, the conditions for choice are larger when the overall wealth in the economy increases.

Let's say a global high-tech bicycle firm, *YourBike*, comes up with an aesthetically stunning bicycle based on customised parts that it produces and assembles in a cost-effective manner in Vietnam. It becomes so popular that it manages to crowd out most of the competition. Small, independent bicycle shops lose business and start closing down. But now, the customer has *less* choice. The entry level price of a *YourBike* cycle is several thousand pounds; simple, affordable city bikes are not made anymore; and small independent bike shops can only survive as a franchise of *YourBike*. Moreover, through clever marketing, customers feel compelled to upgrade their bike every two or three years, and each 10-year-old wants his own smart *YourBike*. Public choice ideologues would argue that, although the market is now dominated by one firm, consumer welfare has increased. Even as fewer people use bicycles (because they cannot afford them), shareholder value, and thus wealth, has grown (Crouch, 2011, 55–56).

The implications of this way of thinking for the position of the giant firm in our economy and society are enormous. We will focus on two: the shareholder value doctrine, and the central position of the large, market-dominating corporation in the political economy of modern capitalism. Customer welfare is hard to establish. Are the customers of *YourBike* really better off when they have to spend a larger share of their income on, admittedly, nicely designed, high quality bikes for their children to go to school? Is society better off when it is more affordable for parents to drive their children to school? These are difficult trade-offs to make, so the public choice ideologues came up with a shortcut: shareholder value. The logic is simple: if the share price goes up, the firm must be doing something right. It has been able to persuade a sufficient number of clients to buy its products and thus increase overall wealth. It also helps that shareholder value is a convenient metric to assess the performance (and income) of managers and for investors and the financial press to assess the performance, or earnings prospects, of the firm. And executives liked it because the share price became tied to their income via generous bonus schemes. It also created short-termism among managers and an excessive focus on quick yields in investment circles.

The second implication is more consequential – institutional or structural, as political scientists are wont to say. Giant transnational firms have come to occupy a central position in the political economy of modern capitalism. Everyone knows that lobbying is big business. Oil companies, big pharma, the airline industry, the financial industry, farmers, all lobby with the EU or the US Congress to influence regulation in their favour. But in the contemporary political economy the concept of lobbying misses the point about the role that the business corporation plays in society. The concept of lobbying assumes that there exists some demarcation line between business on the one hand and a sovereign government on the other. However, according to Crouch, that distinction is no longer very clear. The large global firms that provide the goods that furnish our middle class existence, or our access to the internet and mobile communication, as well as the banks that that provide us with the credit to make those purchases, are as much part of the political-economic order as elected officials and government agencies. Large corporations now have 'systemic importance' for the complex system (in the sense of Chapter 2) of modern capitalism (Crouch, 2011, 122). This insight is as much doctrine as practice, shared by elected officials, administrators, the media and many economists. As we will see below, laws, regulations and fiscal arrangements that favour large corporations ensure that alternatives to corporate hegemony will face an uphill battle.

... and the concomitant decline of small and medium-sized businesses

The rise of the large corporation, in terms of market power, legal clout, and as an object of veneration for politicians, policy makers and the media, was accompanied by a decline of small and medium-sized enterprises (SMEs). In a fascinating and well-researched report, Stacy Mitchell (2016), co-director of the Institute for Local Self-Reliance, describes the diminished role of SMEs in the 21st century US economy. In the report Mitchell shows that between 1997 and 2012, the number of small construction firms declined by about 15,000 and the number of small manufacturing firms by more than 70,000. In the same period the number of local retailers decreased by about 108,000, a drop of 40 per cent relative to population. This process has only been hastened by the rise of Amazon.[1] More ominously, as we will see in the next chapter, the number of community banks and credit unions was cut in half, from 26,000 to 13,000 (Mitchell, 2016, 9). Mitchell makes two powerful arguments. First, she attributes the decline of SMEs mainly to two factors: the anticompetitive behaviour of large corporations that use their power to undermine and exclude smaller, independent competitors. Second, federal and state legislation, that, under the banner of efficiency, stacks the deck against independent SMEs. In Mitchell's words,

About thirty-five years ago, policy makers came to view maximizing efficiency, rather than maintaining fair and open markets for all competitors, as the goal of antitrust. This ideological shift impacted more than antitrust enforcement. It infused much of economic policy with a bias in favor of big business, creating an environment less hospitable to entrepreneurs. (Mitchell, 2016, 4)

This bias in business and fiscal law shows in the precipitous decline in the number of startups in the heartland of capitalist entrepreneurialism. Between 1998 and 2012 the number of startups declined by half. Mitchell speaks of a structural shift in the American economy and concludes that 'the most significant threat to America's entrepreneurs is not technological change or global trade, but rather the rise of an economic and political ideology that has discounted the harmful effects of monopoly power and infused public policy with a bias in favor of big business' (2016, 11). The flipside of the diminishing importance of SMEs is a loss of public value. SMEs are shown to create better value for the communities in which they operate than larger enterprises, provide more and better jobs, create more innovation and stimulate local democracy: 'Sociologists report that, all else being equal, communities with more locally owned businesses exhibit a greater ability to solve problems, and have higher levels of civic participation, including voting' (Mitchell, 2016, 20).

Civil society and economic life

We are now in a position to grasp not only the central position of transnational corporations in modern society, but also the obstacles to the realisation of effective CSR. It is obvious that large corporations are political actors that cannot be avoided or circumvented in our attempts to achieve sustainability or social justice. However, transnational corporations are, to put a more accurate gloss on Theresa May's controversial words, '*organisations* from nowhere'.[2] They are not invested in any community. They are intrinsically cosmopolitan in that they do not identify with any group, community, religion or nationality, except perhaps a generalised urban middle class lifestyle. They operate on a separate virtual continent beyond the reach of national laws and fiscal authorities. They use their technical and financial might to create long complex production chains and transportation routes. The logistics of moving whole production lines from one country to another has evolved into a standard technology. To minimise taxes and maximise profits, they create dozens of proxy companies to write off the costs of the purchase of raw materials or the servicing of internal debt, or to shift profits and debt to low-tax jurisdictions. In order to ensure the smooth functioning of this dispersed, global business megalopolis, they employ scores of business consultants, tax lawyers, banks, international organisations, advertising agencies, and marketing and communication offices. They exploit national tax incentives and corporate welfare arrangements to guide their investment decisions. If necessary, they engage in financial engineering (share buyback, derivates) to artificially increase the price of their shares. In general, national governments are enlisted, enticed, cajoled or, if necessary, threatened to cooperate with them. Business law and fiscal arrangements favour large corporations and put SMEs at a disadvantage. Only the largest, most powerful nations can effectively oppose the large transnational corporation. In a very real sense we have become, what Crouch calls a 'corporation-led society' (2011, 144).

In a way there is nothing new about this argument. Corporations have insinuated themselves into society since the days of mass advertising. The purpose of the ad was, and is, to make the corporation a companiable presence in the life of the individual and the community; somewhat like a friendly neighbour or familiar building at the end of the street. What is different is that the corporation has imposed a new role on the individual. While advertisements try to persuade and leave it to us to acquiesce or not, the modern corporation, using the internet and social media, has actively enlisted the customer. It has appropriated the comforting, aspirational language of community, deliberately confusing the personal and corporate sphere. Corporations such as the sneaker company Nike now 'co-create value' with their customers. Through 'engagement platforms' they identify 'thematic communities' where people exchange 'personal and collective experiences'. Analogous to bottom-up democracy this co-creation of value 'taps into the collective creativity of its customer base' (Ramaswamy, 2008). In the same soothing, motivational spirit, the large corporation communicates its efforts to prevent child labour, improve working conditions, provide a fair return to subsistence farmers, safeguard data privacy, or reduce CO_2 in its production chains.[3] Some companies may even reach the 'do our fair share' level or flirt with 'do no harm' production methods in Kate Raworth's ecologically friendly production scale. We do not want to sound facetious but ultimately, as the Raza Plaza case showed, corporations are governed by the shareholder value principle, which means that CSR inevitably reaches the limits of what the shareholders, rating agencies, equity companies and hedge funds are willing to accept. As we have seen before, seemingly opposite or conflicting strategies do not exclude but exist alongside each other. The rhetoric might have changed but the Friedman doctrine is alive and well.

What are the prospects of real CSR in this situation? How can we realise it? In Chapter 9 we will see that the urgency of collective action to prevent global warming is immense. Time is literally running out to reach our goal of limiting global warming to 1.5°C, the level we should aim for to prevent climate catastrophe. We simply have no manoeuvring room anymore to wait for the glacial pace of evolving CSR to contribute its part. (Sadly, a somewhat wry metaphor in the face of rapidly melting glaciers.) We cannot do without the legal powers of national and supra-national governments, but, as the above analysis shows, government is too implicated in the hyperglobalised economy of transnational corporations to put all of our eggs in its basket. This brings into purview the only sphere outside the purview of markets, corporations or the state: civil society.

The term civil society, as the democratic theorist Michael Edwards argues, denotes not one but three spheres. It points to the associations, independent from state, business and family, in which membership is voluntary (Edwards, 2014, 20). This is the familiar domain of civic associations, NGOs, labour unions, churches, and social movements. The second is civil society as the good life. It denotes the realm of values and norms that form an alternative to, or critical commentary on, the profit-seeking, cynicism and amorality of market, politics and business. Fairness, justice, solidarity, equality, but also 'process' norms such decency, civility, empathy and mutual respect belong to this aspect of civil society (Edwards, 2014, 45). This is the conception of civil society that informs a richer, more inclusive and participatory form of democracy. In terms if this book, it encompasses utopia as a method of imagining a better world. Finally, civil society can be understood as the public sphere. It is a 'non-legislative, extra-judicial, public space in which societal differences, social problems, public policy, government actions and matters of community and cultural identity are developed and debated' (McCain and Fleming, 2000, in Edwards, 2014, 67). In many ways the public sphere is the 'platform' where associations and values meet and connect. It is the sphere where a wide range of voices deliberate, and often clash, and are willing to listen to discuss the shape of collective problems and the feasibility of solutions. If there is such a thing as the public interest, it is likely to be found here, and it functions both as guide to action and a monitor on the activities of state and corporations.

We discussed the concept of civil society to escape from the somewhat claustrophobic quality of the preceding analysis of modern corporate capitalism. There is an alternative, and it has two faces. The first is the social ecosystem of associations and civic values that may include small and medium-sized businesses and community banks. It is a realm of economic life that is not wholly governed and permeated by the money nexus; where personal relations, reputation, and the needs of the customer inform economic transactions. The second is the public sphere: dispersed, anarchic, cacophonic, pulling in different directions. But, imperfect as it is, we have seen that it works. The accords that followed the Rana Plaza disaster were driven by civil society action. As we will see in the next chapter, climate movements such as Extinction Rebellion, #Keep it in the Ground and the Sunrise movement are considerable forces in pressuring governments and business to take the urgency of climate catastrophe seriously. If the utopian reimagination of society has any life left in it, it will be found in these aspects of civil society where community and economy meet. In the 'free spaces' (Evans and Boyte, 1986), away from the state, in which citizens come together and organise themselves, in the norms they evoke to comment on the rough business of politics and corporations, and in their designs for a kinder, more just and sustainable society.

But before we turn to the efforts of civic actors to fight the looming climate catastrophe, we need to discuss another large obstacle: the global finance industry. The freewheeling banking system that we have now will prevent and undo every effort at ameliorative change.

Money as a public good

Too big to comprehend?

As the saying goes: money makes the world go round. In the age of global finance, this truism has a literal ring to it. Societies need capital to finance production. Companies that want to invest in productive activities require money, either by issuing bonds or shares or by taking up bank credit which they pay back at a later date from the return on the investment. Individuals need money to buy essentials or obtain credit to purchase big ticket items such as a house or a car. States provide or underwrite important investments with payoffs that are too uncertain, too big or too far into the future to be attractive to private investors. In general, the development of finance is associated with higher levels of income in the population (Kay, 2015, 3). In addition, lenders need to be protected against the risk of insolvent or fraudulent borrowers. That is why we have banks and some form of state-guaranteed protection of bank deposits. In principle, if not in practice, money is a public good.

However, that is not how banks see it. The financial sector has grown into a global Moloch that, although facilitated by the state at every step, largely operates outside effective democratic or regulatory control. In fact, the banking sector has split off a whole sector, shadow banks, specifically designed to work outside regulatory oversight. The finance sector is an opaque complex of law, customs, policies, trades in IOUs, formal and informal agreements, and personal networks, that is only intelligible to insiders. In fact, its complexity and opaqueness are by design (Huber and Robertson, 2000, 5). The financial sector is rife with conflict of interest and revolving door arrangements (Jenkins, 2020). For example, the governance of the Federal Reserve, the US central bank, is largely in the hands of the same commercial banks it is mandated to regulate (Brown, 2019, 14). The move of government ministers to a lucrative position with one of the major investment banks, or vice versa, is a fairly common career path. The less people understand how these obscure laws, rules and arrangements operate, the better it is for the industry. The public banking specialist Ellen Brown

(2019, 46) maintains that if depositors and investors understood the true costs and risks of banking, they would be less willing to entrust it with their money. Uninterested in economic justice or environmental sustainability (Greenfield and Weston, 2020), banking exerts enormous influence over production, investment, work and the personal lives of countless millions. Wall Street and The City have become symbols of unchecked power, uncoupled from the real economy (Main Street), often working against it. Perhaps because it operates behind closed doors, the financial sector suffers from the incorrigible moral hazard of speculating with other people's money.

Yet, despite its gargantuan size and the bravado of the financial elite, the finance sector is remarkably fragile. In the last 12 years alone, it had to be rescued twice from immanent collapse by huge infusions of public money and state guarantees. And here is the thing. Over the past half century, the production of one of the most important public goods − money − has been devolved to precisely this ramshackle, opaque, dishonest, thoroughly undemocratic, deregulated system of private actors. A system that is mandated to serve shareholder value rather than the public good. And it can only do this by creating debt.

How does this work and what are its effects? Private banks create money by issuing loans. Literally 'out of thin air' (Werner, 2014). When a bank thinks the client is credit worthy it can decide to issue a loan. This involves some strokes on a keyboard that deposits the money into someone's account and creates a liability of the same amount on the bank's account balance. No money has been transferred among internal bank accounts, from the lender's account into the account of the borrower. More than 97 per cent of the money circulating in the economy is created this way. Central banks create cash, which accounts for the remaining 3 per cent of money in circulation.[1]

There are many problems with this way of serving a central public need. For starters, by issuing loans banks create the principal but not the money for interest payments. This is no small beer. If you borrow €100,000 at 3 per cent on a 20-year loan, you pay €165,000 on the principal and €135,971 in compound interest payments. In other words, the €100,000 loan requires over €200,000 in additional money over its amortisation period before it is liquidated. That is money that has to be earned somehow and that does not go into the productive but into the financialised economy. Moreover, this interest step-up is one of the factors that drives the unsustainable permanent growth economy.[2] It is unlikely that the total amount of debt that has been created will ever be paid back. In 2019, total global debt, before the surge in debt because of the COVID crisis, was US$255 trillion, or 355 per cent of global GDP (Tiftik and Mahmood, 2020). This includes different debt categories with different consequences for the debt holders. As we will explain later, government debt is a different animal from household debt.

Second, banks effectively act as gatekeepers to the finance needs of civil society. They can withhold loans to small and medium size businesses, as they did after the financial crisis of 2008, and they can withhold loans to families they deem a credit risk – thereby creating all sorts of equity issues. The privatised finance system is biased towards short-term profits and away from sustainable or socially useful investments. But more importantly, through their pivotal role in the finance system, they make debt slaves of all of us. Citizens, businesses, municipalities, institutions of higher learning and others are dependent for their finance needs on this debt-based system of money production.

Third, private money creation has resulted in a runaway financial sector. The relationship between financial transactions and real economic activity is effectively broken. The value of daily foreign exchange transactions is almost a hundred times the actual daily international trade in goods and services. The value of the collateral underlying the derivative trade (we will come back to this) is three times the value of all assets in the world (Kay, 2015). This is bonkers of course. It goes to show that the finance sector has become a largely self-referential system that makes some people very rich. As the British economist and publicist John Kay concludes: 'The industry mostly trades with itself, talks to itself and judges itself by reference to performance criteria that it has itself generated' (Kay, 2015, 5). And, we should not forget to add, it expects the public to bail it out when it goes through yet another crisis.

It does not need to be this way.

There are many proposals and working examples, now and in the past, of public banks and government-financed social investment programmes. These create money without interest or against very low rates, they channel investment into sustainable activities and social goods; they are banks for the people. Differently put, the ideas, blueprints and working exemplars are available. What is lacking is the will to make them part of the public discourse about money, investment, and democracy. We saw examples of this in the preceding chapter when we discussed the seemingly inevitable decline of community banks. Although almost all of us in one way or another suffer from unnecessary debt or lack of positive investments in our community, it simply does not occur to us that we can change this. A number of powerful intellectual and practical obstacles prevent us from giving these positive ideas and examples the traction they deserve. Taken together the current system's hold on the public mind is so large that it amounts to the kind of hegemonic captivity that we described in Chapter 2.

Although everyone handles money on a daily basis, few people, and that includes professional economists, understand its nature. The same applies to banks and their relationship to money. Or the nature of debt and its role in the economy. There are more than fleeting similarities with organised religion. Every day we perform the same formulaic invocations to the god of money without getting any closer to its mystic core. The high priests of the financial system guard the temples and make sure that its inner working remain invisible to the outsider.

This is not just a matter of cognitive capacity. As we have seen it is not difficult to imagine another financial system. Some innovations in public banking or social investment have been successfully implemented in the past but then overtaken by changes in economic doctrine or killed by adversaries. Some are still in existence, such as the network of local Volks-, Raiffeisen and Sparkassen banks in Germany that play a key role in the country's ecosystem of world-leading medium-sized businesses (BSA, 2000a). The problem is not one of imagination but authority. Such examples of successful democratic monetary innovation simply lack the intellectual clout to multiply and set in motion a transformation of the finance industry.

The practices that sustain the global financial order have entered the most personal spaces of our everyday world – the structure of our everyday life, our personal understanding of money and debt, our career aspirations and our self-image. And even if an individual citizen sees through the hegemonic order, she would be unable to change the system on her own. In our society the possession of a bank account is a de facto token of citizenship. Without it we would not be able to receive payments from third parties, such as employers or pension funds, make payments, to retailers, schools, the tax office, or even prepare our tax return. It would be practically impossible to have a family. It would condemn the individual to a lonesome life on the economic fringe of society, to a pre-modern, barter-economy kind of existence – a step very few of us are willing to take. For all their resilience and communal spirit, none of the modern-day nomads we encountered in Chapter 1 took to the road voluntarily. According to this logic the finance system is vast configuration of nested and interlocked practices that mutually support each other. Try to change one practice and you will run head on into another well-established, unquestioned practice. It is a maze without an exit. This vast web of financial practices gives everyday life and the social-economic order its self-evident character and robs every proposal for change of authority from the start. It draws the boundaries between what is admissible and what is off limits in debates about money and debt.

In such a hermetic situation, institutional transformation requires close collaboration between citizens and authorities. While civil society provides the pressure and ideas for change, authorities design and implement the necessary institutional reconstruction. This is not simple, as we saw in the preceding chapter, but there is no alternative. But before we sketch a fairer and more sustainable alternative to the current financial system, we need to discuss in more detail some of the intellectual and practical obstacles that stand in the way of understanding money and finance. A misguided or mistaken understanding of the nature of money will result in unsound proposals for a reform of the financial system.

Where does money come from?

Although we all use it every day, for most of us the origins of money are as mysterious as the origins of life. Even more astounding is the observation that economists have debated this question for most of the 20th and a good part of the 19th century. Fruitlessly, according to at least one observer, as a surplus of doctrine and a dearth of empirical evidence has led us away from instead if closer to the facts of money creation (Werner, 2014, 12). There are three contending theories about the creation of money and the role of banks. Only one of these, the *credit creation theory of banking* has been empirically confirmed (Werner, 2014). The other two, the financial intermediation and the fractional reserve theory of banking were until recently the more popular.

The *financial intermediation theory of banking* is how the ordinary person, and not a few officials, think banks work. Banks take in deposits from individuals and lend that money to other individuals or businesses who need a loan. They are mere intermediaries, neutral conduits through which money flows, without any influence on the economy. (This is probably the reason that until the financial crisis of 2008, banks did not figure in the models that economists built to predict the behaviour of the economy.) This understanding of banks has a lot of face validity: everyone knows that you cannot spend money you do not have. Right? But then, why has the money supply increased so much over the last few decades? Where has this money come from? The intermediation theory of money does not say anything about the origins of money. For its proponents, money just *is*, like rain, as it sloshes back and forth through the valves and pipes of our economy.

In reality, money is created by private banks. They do this by issuing loans. When a bank extends a mortgage, consumer or business loan, the money shows up – instantly – as a new deposit in the account of the client. But the bank does not need to have earned the money beforehand – they literally make it. Instead of banks waiting for clients to deposit their salaries or savings and then use that money to extend loans, they instead create money by typing some numbers into a client's account. Keystroke money. This astonishing fact has a number of important implications for what we think of as money and for our economy.

Money is not a thing. The numbers on the screen of our laptop that tell us the balance of our bank account *is* money. In today's world money is information, digits in our bank account. Most of us find it easier to hold on to an image of money as coins or paper banknotes, or, better even, something tangible with intrinsic value such as gold or seashells. Most people would be even more surprised to hear that not only is money information, but that strictly speaking, they do not own the money that shows up as numbers in their internet bank account. The bank does. Scores of bank heist movies notwithstanding, there is no room or vault within the bank that holds our money. Instead, the digits on our screen signify a social relationship between the bank and its clients – more precisely a relationship of credit and debt. To understand all this we need to introduce the bank's balance sheets and the all-important concept of liability (Ryan-Collins et al, 2011, 2).

When our bank decides to give us a loan to improve our bathroom, what we, as clients, see is that, let's say, €15,000 is added to our account. What we do not see is what happens in the bank's account ledger. By extending the loan, the bank adds a liability to its ledger (the obligation to credit our account with €15,000) and an asset (our agreement to repay the loan plus interest). Because we can spend the €15,000 by paying plumbers and suppliers of bathroom furniture, the bank's credit is as good as money. In fact, this is what money is. Essentially it is a reciprocal IOU ('I owe you') between the client and the bank (Huber and Robertson, 2000, 24). While we owe the bank the principal of our loans plus interest, the bank has a legal obligation to pay us the money that is in our account. As the American public banking specialist Ellen Brown summarises it, money is not a thing but a flow. 'It is created as an advance against future repayment and extinguished when payment is made' (Brown, 2019, 52).

It needs no comment that, given their money producing capacity, private banks are hugely important. Not only for the proper functioning of our economy but also for the general wellbeing of society and its citizens. We have in effect privatised the production and distribution of money, similar to the privatisation of our energy or water supply. One implication is that, similar to other businesses, the bank's bottom line is to return a profit – to maximise shareholder value. Banks sell credit for profit, and a very handsome one at that going by their quarterly statements.

That is not surprising given the many opportunities banks have to make a profit. First, through the interest they charge on loans. Some observers call interest a 'money tax' because the state could make that same money available to citizens and businesses for free (Huber and Robertson, 2000). Banks usually charge hefty real interest rates (Pettifor, 2017). While these partly reflect the risk of a loan (credit cards usually demand higher rates because of the risk of default and fraud), overall, the proceeds are generous. A second source of income derives from the bank's function as gatekeeper. Banks decide who to lend money to. Those decisions are based on the banks assessment of the borrower's ability to repay the loan, the length of time it takes to recoup (some) of the money, and the ease of making a profit. In practice that means that banks prefer to issue mortgages over business loans, for example. We have seen in Chapter 4 that this practice triggers price inflation in the housing sector. That is not a problem as banks can issue more money in the form of higher mortgages; until the system collapses, as happened in the 2008 financial crisis. That collapse was the result of banks' biggest source of income: investment in the financialised economy, often speculative assets the proceeds of which do not end up in the productive economy. In the financial crisis these were mortgage-backed derivatives in which the bank tried to cash in on information asymmetries by bundling high risk with low risk mortgages, having these so-called 'collateralised debt obligations' (CDOs) certified as low risk by credit rating agencies, and selling them to unsuspecting third parties.[3]

We draw three conclusions from this section on the production of money. First, by handing over the right to issue money to commercial banks the state has relinquished an important public function: democratic control over the allocation of credit. States can of course still decide to invest in sustainable and socially beneficial projects, but in the current monetary arrangement it needs to do that by issuing bonds in international capital markets or by raising taxes. There is a much easier and cheaper way to do this, to which we return at the end of this chapter. Second, the state has renounced the proceeds from issuing money itself. Huber and Robertson (2000, 89) estimate that in 1998 UK commercial banks reaped £21 billion from interest rates alone (base rate plus additional rates for overdraft, minus interest paid out on deposits). They speak of a 'hidden subsidy' to banks; a subsidy that is a prime example of rentier capitalism. Perhaps more importantly, the state, and the central bank, have little control over the amount and purpose of credit that is created by commercial banks. Ryan-Collins et al (2011) show that much of the newly created credit has gone into, what they euphemistically call, 'financial transactions'. This, as they conclude, 'is unsustainable and costly to society, as it amounts to resource misallocation and sows the seeds for the next banking crisis' (2011, 51). And third, by issuing money through extending credit, debt is an inseparable aspect of the contemporary money supply. Because banks create the principal but not the interest, and the additional costs are considerable (as we saw above), debt ineluctably fuels the necessity for continuous growth that is a feature of the current unsustainable capitalist economy.

The hidden order of the finance industry

Commercial banking requires laws, rules and regulations for its proper functioning. As noted, these are often hidden and deliberately complex. (As in difficult to follow, intricate; not in the sense that we discussed complexity in Chapter 2.) Partly, this complexity is the result of collective problem solving. Practical solutions to problems of scale are incrementally welded together to make a large dispersed institutional system function properly. This is the case in the complex system that emerged to regulate the relationship between central and commercial banks. For example, when we transfer £1,000 from our bank A to the account of our friend Bruna in bank B, this transaction flows through the so-called Real Time Gross Settlement (RTGS) system at the Bank of England. This is a system that handles transfers of money by reducing bank A's reserve account and increasing the balance of bank B (Ryan-Collins et al, 2011, 76). With 46 banks that have an account with the Bank of England, 2,070 payment flows and £780 billions of transfers every day (Ryan-Collins et al, 2011, 76), this is a vast calculating machine that is whirring in Threadmill Street to make sure that our bank payments end up in the right place.

This is not all. The RTGS system requires that the participating banks have sufficient reserves with the Bank of England to make sure that they can cover all the transactions that involve them. Central banks have different mechanism to ensure that the system is sufficiently liquid, as it is called in banking terms. An important one is the overnight repo market (see note 4) but it also has a so-called Operational Lending Facility where banks can borrow money for short-term purposes at higher costs than the repo market. The takeaway point here is that it is the activity within the commercial banking sector that determines the size of the reserves that the central bank needs to supply commercial banks. Central banks do attempt to influence the money supply through so-called quantitative easing and other means, but, as we will see, those are blunt instruments.

Much of the regulatory complexity is deliberate, however. For starters, there are not one but two banking systems: commercial banks and so-called shadow banks, large investment banks that operate in wholesale money markets. (These are markets where financial institutions and countries engage in high quantity deals.) Commercial banks are regulated while shadow banks operate largely outside regulation – and have been created for this very purpose. The problem is not only that the regulated and unregulated sector frequently interact, but that many commercial banks also have an investment entity that engages in the same profitable speculative activities as the unregulated sector. It was this mixing of functions that brought big commercial banks such as the Dutch ABN and ING, the British RBS and the Belgian Dexia to, and in some instances, over the brink of insolvency in the 2008 crisis. We all know how the damage was mopped up with large bailouts of public money.

How many people have heard of the repo market or rehypothecation or safe harbour clauses or bail-in rules?[4] What these practices and rules have in common is that they benefit banks, or rather their stockholders and its management, often on a massive scale, and are the result of behind-the-scenes lobbying or downright manipulation. They add up to what earlier in the book we called rentier capitalism, an economy that is aimed at creating exclusive assets that generate income for their owners, instead of innovation and production, let alone the public good.

Designed and deliberate complexity interact in unforeseen ways to create 'real', ontological complexity; unpredictable outcomes that emerge from the interactions between separate elements in the vast, global finance system. For example, the interaction of investment banks and other entities can be a poisoned chalice for the latter. An instructive example is the entanglement of investment banks and national governments in the Euro crisis of 2010. Bonds issued by governments (so-called sovereign bonds) are attractive to banks because they can be used as collateral in obtaining reserve deposits at central banks. Higher risk is factored into the bonds as higher interest rates, which makes the bonds of financially weak countries even more attractive to investors who are chasing yields. At the same time governments have an incentive not to default on their debt. To do so would make it very difficult to find buyers for their bonds in the future and default would most likely also entail lengthy court trials with creditors. The combination of the perceived safety of (European) government bonds and a country's efforts to guarantee its bonds triggers a 'doom loop' of downwards spiralling sovereign and financial risk (Brunnermeier and Reis, 2019, 33). While the banks are bailed out, the affected nation suffers the effects, via a forced sell-off of valuable infrastructure and the imposition of draconian austerity measures on its population. This is what happened in the Greek budget crisis, for example, and it requires little comment that it does not exactly make banks more prudent in acquiring sovereign debt.

The repurchase ('repo') market is where giant financial institutions borrow trillions of dollars from each other and from central banks every day, using securities, often government bonds, as collateral (Fricker, 2018). The idea is to pay the loan back the next day, but often they are rolled over, and rolled over again, and so on. As Mary Fricker, the editor of a website called *Repowatch,* says: 'Every night about $7 trillion is borrowed on the US and European repurchase markets, yet [as we are by now no longer surprised to hear] most Americans have never heard of it because the transactions occur privately among global financial institutions.' (Fricker, 2018) These include the mega-banks, money market funds, hedge funds, mortgage giants Fannie Mae and Freddie Mac, the Federal Reserve, mutual funds, states, municipalities, large businesses, pension plans, mortgage lenders, insurance companies, university endowment funds and some community banks. Differently put, the repo market forms a densely interconnected network of financial institutions. It was the repo market that triggered the financial crisis of 2008.

But wait, was the official story not that it was subprime mortgages that were packaged into exotic derivatives that collapsed when low income homeowners could no longer afford their monthly payments? That is, at best, an incomplete story. Institutional investors lost a lot more money in the 2000 dot.com crisis, yet that did not spiral into a system-wide collapse of global finance. The missing link in the story is the repo market. In the years leading up to the crisis, banks bought large amounts of home loans. Many of these were indeed of the subprime variety. In a process called securitisation they packaged these loans and sold the cash flow (principal and interest) as bonds or as CDOs to other financial institutions, who sold them to other investors, and so on, in long chains of rehypothecation that increasingly watered down the collateral. The banks used the income from securitisation to buy more mortgages. This is important because the large investment banks used mortgages as collateral in the repo market. In Fricker's words:

> Bankers got a repurchase loan, used the repo money to make or buy home loans, used the home loans as collateral to get more repurchase loans, used this new repo money to make or buy more home loans ... and so on. The cycle was very profitable for bankers, but it depended on their going deeper and deeper in debt to their repo lenders. (2018)

It was like a giant game of financial musical chairs with this difference that when the bottom fell out of the market, no one had a chair to sit on anymore. In 2008 repo lenders began to get worried about the lenders' ability to pay and demanded their money back. This quickly morphed into a liquidity crisis that brought the global finance system to a grinding halt.

To let the import of this story, and what it means for the current finance system, sink in, let's briefly return to the way money is created. We saw that in the modern alchemy of money production, keystroke money is transformed into real money. The keystrokes of the bank employee end up as credit in the customer's account who then goes out and spends that money in the real economy, paying the plumber or buying bathroom furniture in our example. One could say that in the interaction between banks and private clients the alchemy is not really alchemy because the client's intention to spend it infuses the keystroke money with the objective to contribute to the real economy. Without that designation the bank official would never have entered the keystrokes in the bank's computer in the first place.

Now let's go back to the repo loans. What we encounter here is the dark side of keystroke money. Repo loans consist of keystroke money with the purpose of obtaining more keystroke money. That keystroke money is then reinvested in securities or derivatives to obtain even more keystroke money, ad infinitum. If, at any one moment, one of the players decides it is a good moment to take their profit and sells their derivatives or CDOs, they will get lots of keystroke money on their bank account with which they can buy a seven-room apartment in Manhattan or a 100-foot yacht. But for long periods of time this wheeling and dealing occurs in the rarefied environment of pure, abstract keystroke money, amassing eye-watering amounts of it. (The process is turbo-charged by the ample use of derivatives; highly leveraged bets on market movements, where the owner is liable for a potential high multiple of his original bet. When Goldman Sachs sold high-interest Greek bonds to investors, it also sold derivatives that bet against the Greek government's ability to pay the interest. So much for conflict of interest.) When the music stops it turns out that the whole process was built on thin air. There literally is no money, in the Main Street sense, to repay each other.

What economists and financial specialists call a liquidity crisis is a misnomer. When in your bathroom renovation the plumber, bathroom store and contractor all want their money on the same day, and your car also needs a big repair, you may not have enough money in your bank account to pay all these big bills, although next month your salary will arrive again. That is a liquidity crisis (unless you have an overdraft facility or another option that allows you to pay your creditors off.) The repo crisis is more of a financial ontology crisis. It is abstractions chasing other abstractions, and the only concrete object that anchored the whole hot air balloon to its moorings, the collateral of a piece of real estate, has been so watered down by many rounds of re-hypothecation, that no one can figure out anymore what part belongs to which security or CDO. The only thing that is real in the end is the O in CDO: obligation. Contracts have been signed and must be honoured if the system is not to disintegrate. (Central banks averted this scenario by distributing huge amounts of keystroke money among the big financial players, to bring back mutual trust.) This, in nutshell, is the anatomy of the financial crisis of 2008.

Mary Fricker and others (Brown, 2019, 116) think that the system risk that is created through the explosive mix of repo-financing, securitisation and leverage has not diminished. Big financial actors are still addicted to repo money furnished by the shadow banks and attempts at regulation have been less than successful or have created new risks (Brown, 2019, Chapter 6). While central banks have been faster and more effective in averting another financial crisis in the wake of the COVID-19 pandemic, their actions have not done anything to remove the ticking time bomb at the heart of the global financial system.

Money as a morality play

Money is the stuff you have in your pocket and that you use to buy an espresso at your neighbourhood coffee shop. But it also the force that brings countries to their knees as in the Asian currency crisis of 1998.

Both the espresso and the currency crisis are about money, but they function in wholly different ways. To confuse them is to make a genre error. A genre error is to judge one category with the inappropriate standards of another. For example, you make a genre error when you criticise the music of the Rolling Stones for its lack of harmonic development as in the music of Bach. They are two distinct musical genres that live by different rules. They are incommensurable.

Most people understand money as the bills in their wallet. If you do not have enough of it, you cannot buy groceries or pay the electricity bill. We know that if you spend more than you earn, you will incur debt. These debts will have to paid otherwise a cycle of reminders, debt collectors, and ultimately personal bankruptcy, kicks in. We know these things so well that a whole moral economy concerning money has emerged. Gil is a spendthrift, but Alex is prudent with money. Saving, planning, investment, industry and forethought are good. Spending money on frivolous things, idleness and waste are bad. Rich people are seen as more deserving than poor people. Populist media cast off those who draw welfare as scroungers or deadbeats. If you sense religious overtones in this, you are not far off.

In his book on money, Jacob Goldstein (2020), the co-host of Planet Money, a popular podcast on US National Public Radio, relates how the gold standard became an issue in the 1896 presidential elections. It was debated with religious zeal. William Jennings Bryan, the Democratic candidate and opponent of the gold standard, delivered what went down in history as his 'cross of gold' speech: '… we shall answer their demands for a gold standard by saying to them, you shall not press down upon the brow of labour this crown of thorns. You shall not crucify mankind upon a cross of gold.' William McKinley, the Republican candidate, and eventual winner of the election was not impressed, Goldstein writes. In defence of the gold standard, he spoke of the 'financial honour' of the government. 'Our creed embraces an honest dollar, an untarnished national credit … Upon this platform we stand, and submit its declarations to the sober and considerate judgement of the American People.' Goldstein concludes: 'McKinley was selling morality more than any economic argument. But instead of Bryan's morality of oppression (by gold) and salvation (by silver), McKinley's was the morality of "responsibility", "duty", and "honour".' (2020, 108–110).

These are not sentiments of a more ignorant and backward time. The morality play over money was re-enacted in the Greek sovereign debt crisis. German media portrayed Greeks as lazy and profligate. The tabloid *Bild* wrote for example: 'Germans were asked "to open the (empty) coffers" and to pay for lazy Southerners. ... Greece, but also Spain and Portugal have to understand that hard work – meaning iron fisted money-saving – comes before the siesta' (Henkel, 2015). These opinions were echoed by more respectable newspapers and German officials, such as then finance minister Wolfgang Schäuble, who chaired the negotiations with the Greek government. And they were anchored in the national pride in the '*Schwarze Null*', as it is called in the German speaking world: the Black Zero, the symbol for the budget surpluses that the German state managed to create year in year out.

Politicians could be forgiven that they understand money as the bills and coins in their wallets. This is what the eco-feminist scholar Mary Mellor calls handbag economics (2016, 20), and more recently the economist Stephanie Kelton, the household myth (2020, 16). The idea is the same: to understand national budgets as if they are similar to household budgets. However, this is not an innocent misunderstanding that ensues from the way we have all been socialised in using money. For starters it so obviously wrong that you wonder why the myth arises in the first place. Everybody, and certainly those who draw up public budgets, knows that governments can print their way out of a deficit while households cannot. But both Mellor and Kelton spend a whole book on refuting the household myth, so apparently the hold over the mind of politicians, economists and the public is stronger than it should. Handbag economics is another instance of the moral economy of money. But as in the battles over the gold standard and over the Greek sovereign debt crisis, morality always serves someone's purpose.[5] In fact, so many strategic misconceptions are packed into handbag economics that it would far exceed the space of this chapter to discuss all of them. Let us touch upon some of the most salient.

Mellor sees handbag economics as a symbol for neoliberal economics that includes market fundamentalism, globalisation, the erosion of worker rights, the perception of taxes as a kind of legalised theft, and governments that have to borrow money from markets or tax citizens and businesses to acquire the resources to dispose of their constitutional tasks (Mellor, 2016, 21). Money is assumed to be a 'limited resource that can only be legitimately used by the wealth creators' (Mellor, 2016, 72). Mellor then relates these ideological beliefs to the practices of commercial banking, in particular the myths surrounding the provenance of money. To counter the strategic ignorance about money, she argues, we should focus on the creation and allocation of money instead of engaging in morally tinged considerations about how individuals and nations dispense it (2016, 53). Money, she says, is in effect a public good that is privately produced. The public, and governments, have little control over the supply of money. And while its purchasing power is backed by the labour, products and resources of people living and working in the real economy (Mellor 2016, 42), banks reap most of the profits of creating money. A central plank of this ideological complex, as we have seen in Chapter 6, is the demand for a small state and the veneration of businesses as paragons of efficiency. Handbag economics is the perfect excuse for austerity.

Debt plays a central role in handbag economics. In the moral economy of money debt is considered a bad thing. Yet, in our financialised society, private debt, although of the responsible kind that is paid back on time, is encouraged while public debt is considered an abomination. This is the moral heart of privatised Keynesianism. In terms of handbag economics, public debt is seen as reckless overspending that incurs tax increases or austerity for the current generation, and saddles future generations with unsustainable financial burdens. Traditional macroeconomic theory portrays the capital markets as a zero-sum game in which government borrowing crowds out corporate borrowing and stifles economic activity. The EU has even enshrined handbag economics in its rules. The Maastricht criteria stipulate that public debt cannot exceed 60 per cent of GDP, and the deficit 3 per cent of GDP.

In her book on Modern Monetary Theory (MMT), Kelton argues that this belief is based on a misunderstanding about the nature of public debt. When the government spends more than it has and incurs a deficit, what happens is that this money goes somewhere. In the giant ledger in which the income and outlays of government and society are registered, government spending is equivalent to society's income. Kelton argues that this flow of money must be seen as an accountancy identity (2020, 106). A government's deficit is society's surplus. And vice versa. Using a simple metaphor of two buckets she concludes: 'Every fiscal deficit makes a *financial contribution* to the nongovernment bucket.' (Kelton, 2020, 107; original italics) Reversely, a government surplus, symbolised by the sacred 'Black Zero' in circles of German (and Dutch and Austrian) policy makers, *reduces* the spending capacity of society. What is triumphantly presented as a fiscal achievement will in effect undermine economic performance. When the government boasts a budget surplus the private sector, short on money, can only continue to invest, pay wages and spend by taking on debt itself. However, in contrast to the state, which is a currency issuer, private sector debt has to be paid back. We have come full circle to the privatised Keynesianism of earlier chapters.[6]

There is one more important misconception to address. Handbag economics is oblivious to financial globalisation. It conceives of nation states as autonomous, clearly demarcated entities. In more than one sense (when you are an immigrant or refugee; when the state borrows money on international capital markets) this is still a good working hypothesis. But, as we saw in the preceding chapter, since the early 1990s the world has entered a period of hyperglobalisation. The effects on a nation's finances are enormous and have little to do with improvident financial morals. Until the 1990s international trade was governed by the remnants of the Bretton Woods regime. Bretton Woods has not always received positive billing by economists, but according to Dani Rodrik (2012) it represented a delicate balance between domestic policy objectives and the possibility to engage in cross-border trade. Or, as he formulates the spirit and substance of Bretton Woods: 'International economic policy would have to be subservient to domestic policy objectives – full employment, economic growth, equity, social insurance, and the welfare state' (Rodrik, 2012, 70). One of the key policy instruments of Bretton Woods was capital controls. In today's globalised financial world, this might seem like an antiquated economic idea, but before 1990 most nations had strict regulations to prevent money moving in and out of the country. While long-term foreign investment was welcomed, short-term lending, borrowing or trading ('hot money') was mostly prohibited (Rodrik, 2012, 90). All this changed with the breakdown of the postwar social pact and the rise of market fundamentalism.

The new consensus was that free transborder capital movements would stimulate global trade and improve the efficient allocation of global resources. This consensus was enshrined in the 1992 EU Maastricht Treaty and the mission and operating routines of international organisations such as the IMF, WTO and the World Bank (the by now infamous Washington Consensus). It would also function as a disciplinary tool for countries that were seen as having lax fiscal and monetary policies (Rodrik, 2012, 104). Differently put, the world was subjected to an unprecedented dose of optimism in the market's ability to self-regulate trade and finance on a global scale. Thirty years later the results of this global experiment are in and they do not look pretty. Economic growth was good but not approaching Bretton Wood levels (Rodrik, 2012, 110). And at what price? Rodrik provides us with a depressing list of financial crises: the Latin-American debt crisis of the

1980s, the currency crises that rocked pre-Euro Europe in the early 1990s, the 'tequila crisis' in Mexico in 1994, the Asian financial crisis in 1997–1998, followed by Russia (1998), Brazil (1999), Argentina (2000) and Turkey (2001). Rodrik refers to a report that lists 124 banking crises, 208 currency crises, and 63 sovereign debt crises between 1970 and 2008 (Rodrik, 2012, 108–109). And that was before the global conflagration of 2008, and now again during the coronavirus crisis. Each of these crises is usually followed by years of economic stagnation and social hardship. The conclusions are clear: unregulated financial markets do not contribute to financial stability (BSA, 2000b).

Rodrik frames the problems with globalisation as a trilemma between unfettered global markets, national self-determination and democracy. He argues that we can only get two out of three of these options simultaneously. We can get global trade and finance and a shot at international democratic arrangements but at the cost of the nation state. Or we can have sovereign states and globalisation, but must forget about democratic self-determination. Or, we have democratically ruled nation states at the cost of unbounded international trade and finance (Rodrik, 2012, 200). The problem is that for the globalised machinery of trade and finance to function, it imposes unrelenting external constraints on the democratic procedure of nation states and the needs of citizens. At the moment the scale clearly tilts towards the hyperglobalisation leg of the trilemma. The signs for this are as familiar as they are dispiriting. The insulation of economic policy making agencies (central banks, regulators, ad hoc crisis bodies, such as the 'troika' during the Greek crisis) from democratic control, the cutback of outlays for social protection and infrastructure and the contracting out of national infrastructure and social protection to internationally operating corporations, the lowering of corporate taxes, the half-hearted attempts at fighting tax havens and corporate tax avoidance, the busy revolving door between politics and the board rooms of large corporations and financial institutions, the demonisation of independent media, and most disconcerting of all, the assault on democratic institutions. And all this is kept in place by a behind-the-scenes regime of international treaties, laws and agreements that overrules national law.[7]

Freely moving capital is incompatible with domestic wellbeing and democratic freedom. The fact that the devastation wrought by cross-border capital is dismissed by economist and politicians as the inevitable costs of the boons of globalisation, is yet another instance of the power of ideology to dull people's moral sensibility. Or, as we phrased it in Chapter 2, the hegemonic power of market ideology.

How to get out of our financial mess

It will be clear that the possibility of a meaningful transformation to a more sustainable and democratic society hinges on a thorough reform of the (global) financial sector. Our analysis of the defects of the current money system contains the seeds for a reform of said system. That reform hinges on four themes: lift the strategic ignorance about the privatised monetary sector, introduce the public creation of money, bring the allocation of credit under democratic control, and impose capital controls.

Educating the public on money

In her book on the production of money the British economist Ann Pettifor (2017) raises a number of important questions about the epistemic dimension of banking. 'Why is there public ignorance about money creation and the monetary system? Who has manufactured this ignorance?' (Pettifor, 2017, 97) We have seen how the global financial sector largely works in the dark. We have also seen that that lack of transparency is deliberate. Pettifor lays part of the blame for the strategic ignorance about money at the feet of 'mainstream economists' (she actually uses considerably stronger language; 2017, 97). But important as the forensic question is, for this book the more important conclusion is that the public, elected officials, public administrators and media professionals must be educated about the functioning and effects of the privatised monetary system and about the outlines of a democratic public alternative.

The first step in a campaign to reform the monetary system is to inform the public. Nothing, except professional parochialism, stops universities from teaching the structure and workings of the global financial system. Newspapers and weeklies could feature items on the benefits of a public banking system. Journalists could educate themselves about the real world of credit and international banking, instead of uncritically passing on the latest oracular statements of central bank presidents. We could harness the awesome power of the advertising industry and the social media to educate the public on the truth about commercial banking and the benefits for society of a money supply that is under democratic control. The first important step is to assail the hegemony about banking and money and create the intellectual space for a public alternative. As Pettifor rightly concludes: 'Fundamental to any attempt to wrest power back from financial markets must be a greater public understanding of the nature

of credit, money creation – and of the monetary system as a whole'
(2017, 130).

The public creation of money

Money is a public good, even in our current privatised system of money
production. As Mary Mellor puts it:

> Contemporary money systems are public because the public,
> taken to be all the people within that money system, are
> affected by, and ultimately responsible for its functioning.
> Money has been created in their name as publicly backed
> currency, that is tokens or records that express a range of
> entitlements or obligations. (2016, 66)

We have seen that money, expressed as digits on a computer screen,
is a relational entity, but that the entitlements overwhelmingly fall
to the commercial banks that issue it (Huber and Robertson, 2000,
iii). Money is a commons that has been subjected to enclosure by
commercial banks. The first step in the reform of the finance system
therefore is to bring the creation of money back under public control.[8]
Technically speaking this is a relatively straightforward operation: instead
of commercial banks bringing money into circulation by issuing credit,
the central bank will enter new (keystroke) money into the current
account of the government (see also Mellor, 2016, 69). This will be
debt-free money. The second step is for the government to bring this
new money into circulation. This step we discuss below under the
heading of credit allocation.

Truly public creation of money has several advantages. First,
governments can control the amount of money they bring into
circulation. They can also control the interest rate, or rates, depending
on the type of investment. This gives them more tools to prevent
inflation. Second, governments will not have to borrow money
anymore – by issuing bonds – to obtain the revenues for public
investment. At the moment, most governments spend between 10 to
15 per cent of their revenue on interest payments, a large chunk of
which goes to foreign bond holders, pension funds, equity companies
or investment banks (Huber and Robertson, 2000, 12). Third, how
governments choose to invest public money is now a matter of
democratic decision making. As we saw, a large part of current spending
is on financial speculation and does not contribute to the productive
economy. However, public money creates the possibility for socially

beneficial, sustainable investment. Obviously, it does not guarantee it. An authoritarian government can unilaterally decide to spend most of it on military, surveillance and police services.

There are different ways to move from the current privatised system of money creation to a public one. Under their proposal for sovereign money reform, Huber and Robertson (2000) envision a gradual phasing out of the right of commercial banks to create money:

> Money will enter into circulation as debt-free seigniorage.[9] So the debt or liability feature of current accounts will disappear, whereas the asset feature for customers will remain – with sight deposits as official means of payment belonging to the holders of the accounts. Thus, sight deposits will become what the amended law will require them to be: plain noncash money – actual money and not, from the banks' point of view, a claim to be repaid money or a liability to eventually have to pay out cash. (2000, 24)

Banks still manage these current accounts, but the money in them is issued by the central bank, debt free. This money is owned by the customer and not the bank, as in the current system. Current accounts are taken off the bank's balance sheets. Under this system banks can still issue loans, against interest, but with money that is issued by a public authority, the central bank. Money is nationalised, but not the banks (Huber and Robertson, 2000, 35).[10]

There are other, less far-reaching models of nationalising money. They usually create a two-tiered system with a publicly funded and a commercial part. The public part can involve one or more public banks financed by debt-free central bank money and more risky commercial banks. The challenge of a two-tier system will be to prevent contamination of the low risk, low yield public system by the fast money of the commercial banks. At the very least this requires strict capital control.

Setting up a system of democratically controlled credit allocation

In her book on the production of money, Ann Pettifor (2017) rightly draws our attention to the role of borrowers in the money creation process. She criticises sovereign money reformers such as Mary Mellor and Huber and Robertson for ignoring the role of investors and consumers in determining the supply of money. Public money reformers focus too much on the supply of money, according to Pettifor, without considering the willingness or reluctance of firms and individuals to invest. 'This approach of focusing narrowly on the money supply ignores what money is lent *for*', she argues (2017). Money must 'work'.

Pettifor has a point here. There is an important distinction between the supply of money (and traditional macroeconomists tend to have a bee in their bonnet about this) and the decisions what to use this money for. One of the major problems of the privatised system of money production is that the state has little control over how it is spent. Once it has borrowed money in the international bond markets or retrieved some of the privately issued credit via taxes, it can decide what to spend it on. But the vast private money supply is largely out of its reach. The state only uses weak instruments, such as lowering interest rates and quantitative easing, to try to influence the total volume of investment and consumption. But these measures only influence the circuit of reserve money and do nothing about interest rates and the credit supply in Main Street.[11] We have seen that banks, on the other hand, have a firm grip of the steering wheel of credit provision. Their strategic credit policy is aimed at high yield, and/or quick yield, and/or low risk investments – in different combinations of these. In practice that means that commercial banks favour consumer loans over loans to SMEs, financial speculation (Wall Street) over investing in the productive economy (Main Street), and the fast money of the carbon industry over the patient money needed for green investment. In addition, the ease of moving capital across borders plays into the hands of speculators who can quickly move capital to high risk, high yield targets and offshore tax havens.

Also, the current two-tier system of money creation, one for citizens and businesses and one for banks using central bank reserves, makes it impossible for governments to specifically target investment. Money that has been 'created' through the central bank's quantitative easing flows into commercial bank's reserves. That money, as we have seen, replenishes the bank's balance sheet but cannot be lend out in the real economy (Sheard, 2013). (Banks can lend the excess reserves to other banks in the repo market or buy assets with it.) Experience has borne this point out. In the economic downturn triggered by the COVID-19 pandemic, it turned out to be almost impossible for the British government, despite providing large inducements, to get banks to lend money to SMEs. It is like pushing with a string.

Also in a public money system, there would be credit and debt. But the difference is that the process of credit creation is less usurious and more democratic. No high interest rates or fees because the bank needs to make a profit. Some public money advocates argue for the creation of publicly financed banks that serve socially desirable goals. Such banks need to be close to the community that they serve. 'Monetizing local credit with publicly owned banks', Ellen Brown calls it (2019, Chapter 8). Her example is the Bank of North Dakota (BND). The BND is financed by the state of North Dakota and functions as a 'bank of banks' of small local banks. It loans to local businesses, to municipalities to finance local infrastructure, guaranteeing liquidity and capital requirements. One important result of this is that local banks can keep these loans on their books instead of having to sell them to Wall Street investors to meet capital requirements. The BND has created an ecosystem of local banks; North Dakota has a higher number of credit unions and small banks – banks that know their customers – than any other state in the US. The BND has been remarkably profitable and has escaped the financial conflagration of the 2008 crisis. Brown explains why:

> Its secret seems to be its very efficient business model. Its costs are very low: no exorbitantly paid executives; no bonuses, fees or commissions; no private shareholders; very low borrowing costs; no need for multiple branch offices; and no FDIC insurance premiums; the state rather than the FDIC guarantees its deposits. (2019, 144)

Moreover, state-financed local banks are good for the state. In 2016, following a collapse in real estate prices, the state and the BND agreed to return $200 million of the bank's profits to the state's coffers: 'BND profits are not siphoned off to Wall Street to be invested overseas or stored in offshore tax havens. They are recycled back into the bank, the state and the community' (Brown, 2019, 144).

The BND is a model for credit allocation in a public money system. The German speaking countries have always had their network of local Sparkassen, Landesbanken and other cooperative banks. As we saw, this made them world leaders in SMEs (Kay, 2015, 169; BSA, 2000a). Their business model is similar to that of the BND: low costs, prudent loans to local or regional businesses, capitalising on relations of knowledge of local markets and trust within the community, long-term loans that enable lenders to pay off the principal without overstretching, and access to the low-cost lending facilities that all banks enjoy (Mitchell, 2016, 14). Yet, despite the wealth of evidence that they outperform large banks on a range of critical measures, they are in decline (Mitchell,

2016). For large, national or international investments countries need a national investment bank, such as the *Kreditanstalt für Wiederaufbau* (Credit Institute for Reconstruction) in Germany, the former Green Investment Fund in the UK (inexplicably sold to private industry in 2017), or the EU's European Investment Bank.

Governments can also issue their own debt. Nothing withholds a government to issue bonds with different maturities and interest rates to investors and the general public. Pettifor draws on Keynes' management of the UK wartime economy to argue for a suite of government issued bonds that are available to the public. For example, it could issue 1-, 5-, 10-, and 30-year bonds for people with different investment objectives (Pettifor, 2017, 140). The benefits of this system are obvious. First, it would open up the bond market to individuals and SMEs instead of maintaining a lucrative monopoly for some equity companies, while the former are relegated to their low interest current or savings accounts with commercial banks. Second, a series of different bonds would make it possible to tailor the financial instrument to the citizen's needs. I might, for example, be interested in buying 30-year bonds as a savings instrument for my retirement. Or I might want to buy five-year bonds at somewhat higher rates to help my daughter set up her internet business. As the state does not need to make a usurious profit the rates are set at reasonable levels. The government does not need to worry about the money supply (apart from tracking where in the economy and to what extent inflation emerges; Fullwiler et al, 2019), as the money is spent in the productive economy, creating jobs and generating taxes.

Impose capital controls

In 1981 in France, the newly elected government of Francois Mitterrand embarked on a Keynesian programme of public sector spending to fight the stagflation that then bedevilled the economies of the West. The government increased public spending to create new jobs, it raised taxes on the wealthy to avoid deficit spending, it expanded social benefits to stimulate demand, and it nationalised major banks to gain control over investment decisions. The reaction of the deregulated international capital markets was swift and brutal: domestic and foreign capital fled France en masse. The government tried to use whatever instruments it had to control the outflow of capital, it devalued the franc several times, but in 1983 it had to give up. After much internal deliberation the government performed a U-turn and imposed a programme of cuts in social spending, increases in interest rates and the abolition of capital controls. The writing was on the wall. The global system of finance would not tolerate any deviation from market ideology (Kuttner, 2018, 76).

It is a tell-tale sign of the power of hegemony that the Mitterrand story has always been depicted as one of a misguided socialist government that ignored the natural laws of the market. Instead, it is a chilling reminder of the hold that global finance has over sovereign nation states. Just imagine the reaction of global capital if a country democratically decides to convert to publicly issued money, and direct national investments towards the green economy while phasing out carbon fuel, and introduce a UBI, and introduce workplace democracy and joint ownership. Globally operating banks, equity companies and hedge funds would simply withdraw their investments in the country, divert it to states with more capital-friendly and worker-hostile regulation, and wait for the collapse of its economy. Their friends in politics and the billionaire press would unleash a media campaign to depict the said country as socialist, communist, or worse. The space for any democratically decided, meaningful transformative change is severely constrained by the unrestrained flow of capital across borders.

In the globalisation trilemma, national democracy always loses. This leads Rodrik to argue unequivocally for restrictions on global finance. 'The rules of the game have to allow for restrictions on cross-border finance designed to counter regulatory arbitrage [12] and protect the integrity of national regulations.' And he continues:

> [T]he responsibility for regulating leverage, setting capital standards and supervising financial markets, would rest squarely at the national level. Most important, the rules would explicitly recognize governments' right to limit cross-border financial transactions, insofar as the intent and effect are to prevent foreign competition from less strict jurisdictions from undermining domestic regulatory standards. (Rodrik, 2012, 264–265)

In the Dutch language we say when someone says something truly outrageous that they are 'cursing in church'. From the perspective of the neoliberal hegemony, introducing national capital controls and the domestic regulation of the behaviour of banks is like cursing in church. Yet, as we have seen, for decades restricting the international flow of capital was a completely acceptable, and accepted, feature of the global capitalist order. More importantly it did not impede economic growth and was compatible with the long period of social and economic stability after the Second World War. None of the reforms that we have proposed so far in this book will be feasible without a reform of the finance system as we have outlined in this chapter. Our collective responsibility is clear: the struggle for a reimagination of a sustainable society, organised for human flourishing, must start with a reform of the (international) finance system.

9

Living in the Anthropocene

A new moonshot?

'This is Europe's man on the moon moment', said EU Commission President Ursula von der Leyen when she announced the European Green Deal in December 2019, just before the COVID-19 crisis hit Europe. Models on economic growth based on fossil fuels are 'out of date and out of touch with our planet', the Commission President said. It was time to develop a new regenerative growth strategy that 'gives more back than it takes away' (Hutchinson, 2019).

The 'man on the moon moment' metaphor is not without problems, for reasons that we will discuss below. But it is instructive in at least one big way: it conveys the sense that something that was deemed inconceivable – namely that a human being would walk on the moon – could be realised. That things that seem beyond human reach can be made possible with human ingenuity, persistence and a leap of faith. We believe that a sustainable society, despite the frequency with which 'Green New Deal' (GND), no growth and other concepts are being mentioned in public discourse, is something that is still not conceivable for many people. It is a dream far removed from what most people think is a realistic possibility. This is despite the fact that the elements and architecture of a sustainable society are well known. Ecological economists have laid out what a society and economy that operates within its ecological capacity would look like (Daly, 1997). There are now several detailed blueprints for how to reach a more sustainable society. Yet, we have been unable to make much progress towards achieving these goals. Why is this the case?

The answer to this question has been obscured by the rear-guard struggles with climate change deniers. Sadly, the amount of attention they receive in the media is inversely related to the tenability of their arguments. Another explanation for the fact that, after a decade of public debate, we are still far removed from even the beginning of a sustainable society is that people are afraid of the costs. They fear not only the end of milkshakes and hamburgers, as former US President Trump keeps telling his followers, but also the costs in terms of jobs lost in carbon-heavy industries and sectors. (The conspiracy myth about the Great Reset, the World Economic Forum's alleged plan to sacrifice human jobs and lives at the altar of reducing carbon emissions, is an extreme variant of this fear.) But this explanation does not go far enough. The cost of people having to change their lifestyle and losing their jobs are acceptable to politicians for goals that are far less pressing than averting a climate catastrophe – such as limiting the public deficit.

A better argument, but still not sufficient, is political obstruction. There is no doubt that financial and corporate actors who have a stake in the carbon industry have the ear of politicians worldwide. The amount of lobbying money spent on supporting oil, mining and polluting industries defies belief (Laville, 2019). Similarly, through (often hidden) subsidies and loopholes, carbon-dominated businesses rake in billions in corporate welfare (Reyes and Balanyá, 2016) from states and supra-state actors such as the EU. Banks and insurance companies still heavily invest in industries that destroy the climate (Greenfield and Weston, 2020). Yet, we think that the difficulty in making the transition to a green society is above all the result of being caught in a complex system of institutionalised practices and routines that, taken together, sustain the neoliberal, extractive world order – and that makes an alternative inconceivable. These are the combined effects of complexity and hegemony, as we laid out in Chapter 2. Our first task, then, is to take a step back to recognise the many ways in which a particular practice hangs together with, and mutually supports, a range of other practices.

Conceiving human survival

Since we have started working on the ideas that led to this book, back at the beginning of the COVID-19 crisis in March 2020, some of the themes and positions that we argue for have gained momentum. Even many liberally minded people now call for the state to strengthen our healthcare systems, solve the housing crisis, and support people's livelihoods. Forms of unconditional and basic income have become a hotly debated topic in many countries (see Chapter 5). The climate catastrophe is different. The more we have had to worry about our immediate needs, such as job and income losses, and providing care for our children and ill or elderly relatives, the more the climate crisis seems to have moved into the background of our minds. To give an example: a representative survey of the Austrian population showed that Austrians, even only three months into the crisis (late May 2020), were less supportive of measures to protect the climate than they were before the crisis. This applied particularly to those who had suffered income losses. Moreover, the longer people had been affected by reduced work hours, the less concerned they were about the climate. Higher formal education, in contrast, correlated positively with climate consciousness. At the same time, a majority said that government should take measures to battle the climate crisis rather than holding individuals responsible (see also Kittel et al, 2020).

It is plausible to assume that, in the ongoing crisis, people feel overtaxed; it is simply too much for people to worry about the climate going up in flames when they do not know how to pay their rent, how long they can keep their business afloat, or mourn the death of a loved one. This is true particularly when your country is not one on the battle lines of climate change. But it may also be that many of us sense what Kate Aronoff and colleagues describe in their book *A Planet to Win* (2019) that something *fundamental* needs to shift in how we think and act with regard to climate change and the natural environment. This 'fundamental shift' comprises two things. Let's call them the Grand Narrative and the Modest Story. The first is a new Grand Narrative that enables us to see that the things that we, in the rich world, have done so far to fight climate change are not enough. 'Change your lightbulbs ... Plant a tree when you fly. Turn your lights off for an hour a year. The name of the game was always the same: show people how they can change without changing much of anything at all.' (Aronoff et al, 2019, xii) But if people had changed their behaviour in more fundamental ways, if they had been able to leave a much hated job that they also need to commute to for several hours a day, and if they had stopped believing that rest and relaxation must take place at a beach or a shopfront in a faraway country, it would have hurt important business interests – this is one of the reasons that it has not happened. If we want to successfully tackle climate change, we need to hurt at least *some* business interests – namely those businesses that profit from the destruction of the planet. (The neighbourhood café, the hair salon and even the local sawmill suffer much more from climate change than they would from the 'costs' of creating a sustainable economy.) We need to change how we do things, what purposes we do them for, and how we measure success. As Aronoff and colleagues (2019, 5) soberly summarise, '[u]ltimately, capitalism is incompatible with environmental sustainability'. This is the story that fills a large part of this book. It is the story of how to make public policy and how to do it better. It is a story we recognise and are familiar with, even when we disagree with parts of it.

The second one, we call it the Modest Story, is about our everyday relationships with the natural world, the place where we live (as the conjunction of a specific physical fabric and a repository of meaning), our community, our next of kin, and ourselves. Although made up of small practices, ultimately this story of humble acts has more far-reaching, hegemony-challenging implications than the Grand Narrative. And, although it concerns everyday, commonplace events, in its implications it is more confrontational and less comfortable than the Grand Story. The Modest Story depicts a world of flows and distributed agency in which we are immersed, whether we acknowledge it or not. No one captures this better than William Connolly when he says:

> The agenda is neither to reduce humanity to the rest of nature conceived as lacking all creative power nor to supplement a human will divided against itself with divine grace. It is to appreciate multiple degrees and sites of agency, flowing from simple natural processes, through higher processes, to human beings and collective social assemblages. Each level and site of agency also contains traces and remnants from the levels from which it evolved, and these traces affect its operation. (2011, 22)

Connolly speaks of 'distributed agency'. He uses the language of complexity theory. But, unlike many complexity theorists, he infuses it with human intention and endeavour. The key word in the long quote above is 'appreciate'. We are not just cogs in a vast machine of complex processes, but agents with needs, values, appreciations, sympathies and antipathies, goals, desires, and spiritual needs, who move about in these intersecting flows of energies, materials and ideas. We inflect and experience these flows, in constructive and destructive ways, on minute and dramatic scales, in different registers of temporal development. We constantly navigate a dynamic environment of affordances and constraints brought about by the flows and system states that emanate from other scales of organisation. As Connolly realises, for such a world we have 'no fully adequate conception of human agency available to us today' (Connolly, 2011, 22) We do not quite know how to know, act and value in such a world of complexity and distributed agency – fundamentally a world of becoming.

We do not pretend that we have the answer to this conundrum, but part of the exercise in utopian reimagining that this book represents is to formulate problems in an interesting, generative way and suggest ways forward. This is where the agenda that Connolly refers to comes in: to imagine an embedded agency that respects the dynamic, multi-layered, interconnected world of becoming. To harness such a world, we could do worse than to listen to indigenous knowledge. In a remarkable article, tellingly titled *Land as Pedagogy*, the Nishnaabeg activist and scholar Leanne Betasamosake Simpson (2014) presents the outlines of indigenous ways of knowing. Introducing Kwezens (literally 'little woman'; Simpson, 2014, 2), a small girl collecting firewood in the woods, Simpson describes how indigenous knowing proceeds from careful and patient observation of the surrounding world and drawing conclusions from it. Kwezens watches a squirrel in the tree under which she rests suck on the tree's bark. Her curiosity piqued, she imitates the squirrel and tastes a sweet liquid. She has discovered maple syrup. She relates her discovery to her grandmother who tries out the syrup in cooking. In the end the village collects the juice from the trees.

The maple syrup story show how knowledge is experiential, embodied and relational. '[Kwezens] learned both from the land and with the land', Simpson says. But her learning trajectory is also communal, moved forward by the encouragement and trust that her elders bestowed on her. Learning is the combined achievement of family, community and context (Simpson, 2014, 7). Simpson contrasts Kwezens' learning with the regular education programmes she was enrolled in: 'coping with someone else's agenda, curriculum, and pedagogy, someone who was neither interested in my well being as a kwezens, nor interested in my connection to my homeland, my language or history, nor my Nishnaabeg intelligence.' (2014, 6) This negative contrast is not just a rhetorical trope to accentuate the virtues of indigenous knowing. Simpson describes the universalising, reductionist tendencies of western knowledge and the disengaged organisation of teaching that is culturally imposed on students and inquirers alike. Just look, by way of contrast, how Simpson describes conceptualisation, generalising from careful observation, in the indigenous mode:

A 'theory' in its simplest form is an explanation of a phenomenon, and Nishnaabeg stories in this way form the theoretical basis of our intelligence. But theory also works a little differently within Nishnaabeg thought. 'Theory' is generated and regenerated continually through embodied practice and within each family, community and generation of people. 'Theory' isn't just an intellectual pursuit – it is woven within kinetics, spiritual presence and emotion, it is contextual and relational. It is intimate and personal, with individuals themselves holding the responsibilities for

finding and generating meaning within their own lives. ...
Most importantly, 'theory' isn't just for academics; it's for
everyone. ... 'Theory' within this context is generated from
the ground up and its power stems from its living resonance
within individuals and collectives. (2014, 7)

We quote Simpson at length here, because this remarkably subtle
and rich evocation of the role of 'theory' in Nishnaabeg knowing
amounts to no less than an alternative epistemology. Theory,
knowledge is narrative, and thus embodied, guided by emotion and
tradition. It is holistic and relational in that it takes past and future
generations into account. In the Nishaabeg's relationship with their
environment, knowing is always actionable, emerging from and aimed
at practical understanding of the situation at hand and guided by a
holistic understanding of its relationship to the community, natural
environment and past and future generations. Nishnaabeg knowing
contains a subtle ethic of positive engagement with the environment,
as well as a certain humility in the face of its ever-present potential
for change and surprise. Indigenous ethics is not an afterthought to
disengaged knowledge, it is not divided from it. Instead it is a form of
affectionate knowing in its own right that shapes attention and guides
the course of humans through the world. Nishnaabeg knowing is a
way of going about that is ultimately suited to a dynamic world of
intersecting flows and unpredictable outcomes.

Remarkably, this indigenous knowing strongly resonates with
another subaltern epistemology: practice theory. We introduced the
concept of 'practice' in Chapter 1 and, in the course of the argument
there, depicted entrenched, habitual personal and collective practices
as obstacles to change. Suffice to say here that practices do not
only act as constraints but, in fact, make it possible for our formal
institutions to function at all. Practices are the taken-for-granted,
routine, embodied intelligence, suspended between generations,
that hold our organisations, laws, and policies together (Cook and
Wagenaar, 2012; Freeman, 2021). But far from being simple mindless
routines, practices can better be compared to the microbiome in our
body, the living, adapting ecosystem of microbes that are essential
to our body's functioning and connect it to the wider world. In a
similar way practices are the tacit ecosystem of activities that connect
personal skill and understanding to wider cultural patterns. The aim
of practice is not certainty and control but attentive adaptation to ever
changing situations. Practice, like indigenous knowing, is relational
and embodied. Yet, despite the intrinsic role of practice for our

economy and society, it plays a subordinate role in science, management and education.[1]

Dealing green

The Green New Deal – the American Version of the path to sustainable societies – borrows its name, and its promise, from Franklin D. Roosevelt's comprehensive package of reforms initiated during the 1930s. With the New Deal Roosevelt sought to bring the nation back on track following the Great Depression (of which an important cause was a banking crisis). Best known for the '3 Rs': economic *recovery*, *relief* for the unemployed, and *reform* of the banking system, the New Deal was a major transformation of key institutions, including monetary reforms such as the famous abolishment of the gold standard (meaning that the dollar was no longer convertible to gold).

The invention of the term 'Green New Deal' (GND) is commonly attributed to the centrist American writer Tom Friedman. In an op-ed in the *New York Times* in 2007, he argued that the time was ripe for an approach to tackle climate change. We need to treat the world as a place where all things are connected, Friedman argued, and thus our solutions need to concord with this complexity: 'If we are to turn the tide on climate change and end our oil addiction, we need more of everything: solar, wind, hydro, ethanol, biodiesel, clean coal and nuclear power – and conservation' (Friedman, 2007). In the United States, the Obama administration approached this vision only in homeopathic doses, assuming that, to tackle climate change, one needs first to get business on board. But thinkers and politicians endorsed wide-ranging programmes that combine environmental, social and racial justice.

Perhaps the most prominent articulation of this framing stems from Congresswoman Alexandria Ocasio Cortez' programme for a GND, which she released in the form of a 14-page document in 2019. In it, she did not portray the climate crisis as merely an environmental catastrophe. Instead, she pointed towards its intimate connection with social, economic and racial inequality. 'Climate change, pollution, and environmental destruction' the document says, 'have exacerbated systemic racial, regional, social, environmental, and economic injustices … by disproportionately affecting indigenous peoples, communities of color, migrant communities, deindustrialised communities, depopulated rural communities, the poor, low income workers, women, the elderly, the unhoused, people with disabilities, and youth' (US Congress, 2019). The proposed solution is a decade-long, wide-ranging programme of political, social, and economic reforms to achieve the following aims: net-zero greenhouse gas emission, fairly paid jobs and economic security for all, and large investments in the environmental, social, and economic sustainability of US infrastructure and industry. The programme also calls for action to ensure that everyone, now and in future generations, has access to clean air, water and nature, climate and community resiliency, healthy food, and a sustainable environment. Last but not least, the document highlights the need to 'promote justice and equity by stopping current, preventing future, and repairing historic oppression' of disadvantaged ('frontline') communities (US Congress, 2019).

Despite being mostly a programmatic statement, without charting a path towards implementation, Ocasio Cortez' proposal is one of the more radical visions of a sustainable society. As such, it goes against the interests not only of the carbon and coal industry but also against many of the (legal or de facto) entitlements of big business. It demands the mitigation of the stark inequalities along social and racial lines. Its call for institutions and policies to change towards a more just distribution of power and resources may be threatening to those whose privilege merely derives from social hierarchies grounded in tradition and familial influence. No wonder, then, that Ocasio Cortez' plan was attacked as too radical and ridiculed as a utopian wish-list that is out of touch with reality. Some news outlets simply called it 'crazy' (Haskins, 2019).

For others, however, it is not radical enough. Among them are many young people who fear for their future. In a podcast episode on 'Generation Green New Deal,' 22-year-old student and climate activist Nikayla Jefferson describes how her 11-year-old brother does not believe he will make it to old age because of the climate catastrophe. When she hung out at the beach with her friends in San Francisco in 2020, Nikayla recounts, they needed to wear masks to protect themselves against the smoke from large forest fires (Generation Green New Deal, 2020). People like Nikayla and her brother have a different sense of urgency from the people who run their country. What seems inconceivable for most older people, namely that we need to radically change our economy and our own way of living, seems common sensical to them. They have been growing up in a world in which safe housing is not only a social issue, but also an environmental one. Safe housing means that one's home can withstand floods, bushfires and storms. Nikayla and her brother, alongside many others, do not only know, but also *feel* and *experience* – in a big-city variant of the indigenous knowing we described above – how deeply intertwined the climate crisis is with the social and economic justice crisis. Addressing one will not work without tackling the others. They are acutely aware that the time for incremental solutions has run out. Effective climate policies are radical policies (Aronoff et al, 2019, 18).

Gardening, not engineering

We believe that the comprehensive, interconnected way in which many proposals and visions of the GND describe problems and suggest solutions is one of its most radical features. And it also helps to explain why so little progress has been made to achieve it. We cannot simply fix the problem with solutions that focus on changing individual behaviour, such as putting solar panels onto our roofs or subsidising electric cars. We need to change not one thing but many. We believe that we cannot do this without having a new concept of how things not only hang but also develop together, and of our place, as humans, in this interconnected web of flows, energy and materiality. We need a distributed conception of agency, as William Connolly calls it. If we learned one thing in the past two decades, it is that the complexity of climate change is dynamic, evolving complexity. Thus, we need a new metaphor. And this is where we return to the 'moonshot' analogy at the beginning of the chapter. By using that phrase, EU Commission President von der Leyen not only appealed to people's sense that we can try to make the impossible happen, but she also framed the quest for a sustainable society in a particular way: as an engineering project.

The concept of engineering is, of course, closely associated with many of the achievements of the last 200 years: electrification, pharmacology, information and communication technologies, and machines revolutionising agriculture, transport and education. And its spell reaches far into the 21st century, where we continue to set our hopes in engineering solutions for a wide variety of societal challenges such as battling disease (in the form of tissue or genetic engineering) or fighting climate change (geoengineering). As is well known, engineering is the application of scientific knowledge to artefacts (such as machines, software, or physical substrates such as genes) that intervene into the world. It is typically distinguished from science by its focus on using, not testing or generating, knowledge. And it is different from art by its systematic commitment to the properties of materiality and the laws of science and mathematics, instead of the wild leap of imagination.

Moreover, if we look at some of the most awe-inspiring engineering projects in our world – the Pyramids of Giza, the Oslo to Bergen railroad, the Delta Flood Management complex in the south-west of the Netherlands, the Large Hadron Collider – we find that they are all feats of human mastery over the material world. They enable humans to scale the mountains by train, push back the sea, peer into the cosmos and cure a disease. This notion of human mastery is not only reflected in the projects that 'big engineering' has tackled, but also in its very principles. Engineering hinges upon precision and the ability to predict – to calculate precisely – how a tool or machine or system will behave and the impact it has on the particular slice of the world on which it operates. This, in turn, means that the engineer needs to not only know all the elements and factors that can impact the operation of the machine and the system, but they also need to be in control of them.

But we cannot be 'in control' of the planet. Neither can we be in control of the climate – it is a complex system that we are indelibly connected with, that perhaps we can harness, but that we cannot, and should not, attempt to master. No matter how much engineering has helped to increase prosperity and progress in the world, and how helpful the engineering metaphor has been in driving home that human ingenuity and perseverance can successfully tackle the most difficult challenges, in connection with creating a sustainable society, it sends the wrong message. The universalist, reductionist way of knowing can only bring us so far. We cannot escape complexity – which is something that indigenous knowing, as well as practice theory, captures. Instead of more engineering, we need more gardening.

A good engineer should have a high level of logical and analytic thinking, a knack for maths, and a focus on problem solving. A good gardener, however, needs different skills: the ability to observe, 'listen to' (sometimes, quite literally), and learn from nature. Gardening is not mastery, but relation. Despite the most well informed and precisely planned attempts to create a garden in a specific design, it is impossible to plan a specific outcome at a drawing board and merely 'implement' it. Because the gardener cannot control all the elements that will have bearing on the outcome, they need to work with a certain level of uncertainty. This is why some people say that gardening is the healthiest form of gambling: the gardener can analyse the soil structure, know everything there is to know about plants, consider the principles of garden design, and precisely dose irrigation. Even equipped with such knowledge and tools, they will only be able to create a garden that comes close to the design in their head – but they will never know the outcome exactly. They cannot foresee how the temperature, the wind, the insects, parasites, and other factors that shape and inhabit a garden will behave. A gardener is tending to a garden rather than engineering it. They are in a dialogue with nature. They can sow the seeds, plant the seedlings, or tear out the weeds, but they can never fully be master.

This is, we believe, how we should go about building a sustainable society. Like a good gardener, we need to ensure that we have good soil, that we plant things that can grow in this soil, and ensure that the garden has access to sun, water, and anything else that it needs to grow. And then we need to observe, tend and learn from the plants that are growing, and the animals that inhabit the garden. This does not mean to throw our hands in the air and say: the climate is so complex, we cannot do anything about it anyhow. It means to harness complexity.

In her book *Braiding Sweetgrass* (2013), the American ecologist Robin W. Kimmerer describes how she had learned from her parents and grandparents to listen to the stories that plants had to tell. Upon entering university, her education in plant biology taught her to unlearn the attentive skill of hearing and train her analytical skill of seeing. 'I honor the strength of the language [of science] that has become a second tongue to me', she writes. 'But beneath the richness of its vocabulary and its descriptive power, something is missing. ... The language that scientists speak, however precise, is based on a profound error in grammar, an omission, a grave loss in translation from the native languages of these shores' (Kimmerer, 2013, 48–49). These words are not merely a critique of the reductivism of science, but a call to complement the grammar of precision, mastery and control with a grammar of interconnectedness (Kimmerer calls it 'a grammar of animacy'), which inevitably entails an openness for the unexpected, and for that which we do not yet know but have to learn from others.

Like Simpson, Kimmerer draws upon a traditional way of knowing, seeing and relating to the natural environment common among many indigenous people. It involves an education of our senses and a reframing of our relationship with the natural and social world. The world, and our presence in it, is understood as process and connection. It requires a different attitude towards time, not the punctuated hypertime of modern capitalism but the deeper, slower time of growth and development. And the embracing of values of humbleness, compassion, balance and joy, where we open ourselves to learn from nature instead of imposing ourselves on it for our short-term exploitative goals.

While writing these lines we hear the nagging voice of human mastery in our heads. Openness to surprise and the unexpected, isn't that risky? We have a decade to get climate change under control – otherwise the human race may not survive. Should we not try to plan exactly each step of the way, rather than plant the seeds and watch things grow? But there is a problem in the way that this question is posed – getting climate change 'under control' tries to do too much and too little. We need to build a society that enables humans to live in such a way that they do not kill other species, and each other, in the process. The Grand Narrative and the Modest Story need not be in conflict with each other. We need every bit of technological insight and innovation that we can muster to understand and measure climate change, design renewable energy sources, phase out carbon fuels, stop the loss of biodiversity and the erosion of our soil, and deal with the fallout of global warming. But we should be guided by holistic and relational ways of knowing. The concept of the Anthropocene signifies that human activity is entangled with the rest of the Earth in a multitude of ways: through geological, meteorological, chemical, zoological and virological phenomena and relations. The COVID-19 pandemic is an example of this. Against this backdrop, a standalone 'moonshot' project to address climate change is a fatal misunderstanding. Instead, science and technology should be integrated in an *ethics of gardening*: guided by attentive observation, by openness to the environment and our place in it, by receptiveness to the effects of our interventions, by respect for the needs and understandings of other stakeholders, including non-human ones. Instead of mastery and control (see also Caduff, 2020), this is a joint process of 'coming to know', as Lianne Betasamosake Simpson states it:

> Coming to know is the pursuit of whole body intelligence practiced in the context of freedom, and when realized collectively it generates generations of loving, creative, innovative, self-determining, inter-dependent and self-regulating community minded individuals. It creates communities of individuals with the capacity to uphold and move forward our political traditions and systems of governance. (2014, 7)

We need to start with digging up the foundations of our society, and plant the seeds for a better one. And then: tend, watch, learn.[2]

Towards an ecological society

When thinking about how to move closer to a sustainable society, key thinkers have proposed policies and approaches that almost always contain the following elements: a steady state economy and the abandonment of the growth delusion, a needs-based instead of wants-based economy, a return to more localised production and exchange and the abandonment of unregulated international trade, a labour intensive economy, and better monetary and fiscal coordination. In the final section of this chapter, we briefly outline the aspects that, within each topical field, we believe to be the key measures. We will also outline what we need to keep in mind when we see the quest to create a sustainable society a project of gardening and not engineering.

No carbon economy

The world's energy sources need to become clean and sustainable. We use this phrase only sparingly, but if we want the human species to survive, there is no alternative to saying goodbye to carbon. A global justice dimension is key here: countries that struggle making the necessary investments into clean infrastructures and economies need to be supported by the international organisations that now sustain our hyperglobalised economy. Moreover, because our reliance on carbon so far has already created problems, we also need to spend resources on mitigating these. This will include training people to respond to environmental disasters such as floods, fires and storms (Aronoff et al, 2019, 87). Another important aspect is that, regardless of what wonderful aspirations programmes and policies state, if countries do not bid farewell to the fetishisation of economic growth, the implementation of any attempt to replace carbon with clean energy will necessary sabotage itself.

Clean air, water and soil

Access to clean air, water and soil, was something taken for granted for so long that it never found its way into human rights catalogues. This does not mean, however, that it should not be considered a human right: it plays a central and enabling role for almost all other rights and capabilities, including people's right to physical integrity. Developing high-tech solutions for cleaning air, water and soil, as well as quality monitoring, are useful approaches, but they still follow the engineering paradigm. To complement these by instruments from the gardening toolbox, we suggest placing even greater emphasis at avoiding pollution in the first place. Mobility should be increasingly collective and emission-free, farming should be sustainable, industrial animal farming should be phased out. Whenever pollution taxes are levied, these need to be calibrated in such a way that they burden large corporate polluters and do not penalise people or households that pollute because they do not have a choice, for example, because an inexpensive car is their only way to get to work or to school in the absence of good public transportation.

Job creation and economic development

As noted, all attempts to create a greener and more sustainable society will fail if our understanding of economic development does not change as well. We need economic indicators that measure factors that contribute to the flourishing of people and societies, and the protection of other species and the ecosystem. We argued in Chapter 5 that the cooperative model creates a stakeholder model that is much more attentive to the needs of the embedding community and environment than the public limited company. (It is also a great expression of a richer, more participatory form of democracy.) In Chapter 7 we argued that small and medium-sized businesses are more attentive to the social and ecological needs of the communities in which they operate. In connection with the creation of new jobs – both to support the transition into a more sustainable society, and to support the meaningful engagement and livelihood of people – we are inspired by Pavlina Tcherneva and colleagues' focus on a care initiative. We need jobs that care for the environment, for the community, and that care for people (Tcherneva, 2018, 8; see also Chapter 5). A society of cooperatives, and a focus on supporting SMEs instead of giant, transnational corporations, would make such a green job guarantee programme much easier to realise.

Social security

In Chapters 3, 4 and 5 we presented the basic elements of our vision for what a social safety net for contemporary societies should look like. We called it the bread-and-butter model, whereby the most substantive part (the bread) consists of well-funded public services and infrastructures that satisfy most of people's basic needs, including social and health care, housing, education, transportation, and information. The 'butter', we believe, should consist of an unconditional basic income that ensures that nobody needs to live in poverty. We also support job guarantee programmes, albeit not as a universal right for everyone (for reasons that we explained in Chapter 5) but as a targeted instrument for specific population groups, such as women after maternity leaves or older people seeking employment.

Money

As Ann Pettifor has convincingly demonstrated, the ability to install capital controls to stem cross-border flows of capital is a condition for financing a green economy. Without such controls global financial finance will simply withdraw capital from a country and drive up interest rates to make borrowing prohibitively expensive. Similarly, the application of antitrust laws should lead to the regulation of a globally operating corporate sector that evades national laws and taxation schemes and uses its wealth to influence susceptible politicians to do its bidding.

Yet, a listing of the different elements of an Ecological Society, important as it is, somehow misses the point. In the next chapter we will show that the concept of *Ecological Society* is shorthand for a vision that inspires and guides the transformation that we describe in this book. Ours is the age of Anthropocene (Pálsson, 2020). The term Anthropocene is associated with climate breakdown and the gradual destruction of our natural environment. In this book we use the method of utopian thinking to reimagine the Anthropocene. Instead of a negative concept we prefer to see it as a positive aspiration. There is no getting away from the impact of humans on the natural environment. Pálsson (2020, 10) says: 'Not only have we become a dictating factor, we have become part of geos, the Earth itself. Everything is both geologic and human at the same time.' We can acknowledge this fact and, in the spirit of gardening, begin to use our entanglement with the natural environment as a positive force. We assert that we can turn our negative impact on our natural environment into something beneficial and regenerative. For this we need to think, see and feel differently about the natural and social world we live in. We argued that indigenous knowing might function as a guide towards such a transformation. The metaphor of gardening is an attempt to extend this kind of relational, developmental thinking to the world of politics and public policy.

The crisis sparked by the COVID-19 virus has shown how destructive and unjust, and ultimately unsustainable, the current political-economic order is. All the elements presented in this book – good public infrastructure, affordable and accessible housing, sufficiently remunerated and democratically anchored work, good government, a responsible business sector that acknowledges its debt to society, and public finance, are all necessary to make the transition to a society and economy that lives within its ecological and economic capacity and respects the social floor below which it cannot sink. Although to the everyday citizen institutions appear as immutable and unassailable, they are not hardwired into reality. Institutions are a mixture of relatively static laws, rules and organisations on the one hand, and articulations of norms, values and meanings about issues that citizens or officials consider important or urgent on the other. That is, institutionalised practices can be subjected to inquiry and debate. They are human-made and they can be changed.

10

Towards an ecological society

Be realistic: demand the impossible! (1968 slogan)

By way of a vision

When we were writing this book, we were facing a dilemma. We were certain that what the world needs is usable knowledge and workable solutions to address a series of urgent problems that have been laid bare by the COVID-19 pandemic. However, we were torn between presenting workable, tested policies and an urgent, inspiring vision. While it makes sense to focus on concrete solutions to society's problems, just outlining policies threatens to regress into a shopping list without an inspirational idea that holds it together. It shackles the badly needed utopian imagination. It risks 'binding "real" or "viable" utopias too close to the present' as Ruth Levitas says (2013, 148). The well-known legal scholar and activist Robert Unger (1998, 4) puts it as follows:

> The public intelligentsia ... insist upon the supremacy of technical policy analysis and practical problem-solving by experts. Yet, this programmatically empty and deenergized politics fails to solve the practical problems for whose sake it renounced larger ambitions. It slides into drift and impotence because it allows itself to degenerate into short-term and episodic factional deals, struck against a background of institutions and assumptions that remain unchallenged and even unseen.

Unger says here that an exclusive focus on technical solutions, important as these are, entails both a loss and a risk. Focusing on getting things done risks embracing what we called in the preceding chapter the engineering approach to climate change – exemplified by the 'moonshot' narrative promoted by the EU Commission president. Slowing down global warming, reforming the global finance system, providing affordable housing, and so on, require large amounts of technical expertise. But these are not isolated, standalone problems. By seeing them as 'just' technical problems we lose a relational understanding of the issue at hand. Societal problems are always embedded in a wider context of beliefs values, meanings and practices. They also hang together in complex ways, as we argued throughout this book. By ignoring or denying this, as Unger says, you risk being left emptyhanded when your preferred solution fails – as it is likely to do in a world of complexity. Moreover, and this is the background to the 'moonshot' metaphor, technical solutions rarely challenge the assumptions on which our institutions, and thus our problems, are built. Doing that would make the issue much more potent and controversial, yet also open up new possibilities for genuine change.

We have seen how important a vision was for the politicians of Red Vienna. Their progressive-humanitarian ideal of elevating the working classes guided and integrated the many policy measures in the field of housing, public health, childcare, architecture and public art. Their vision also articulated a cause that energised a wide range of people who were willing to devote time and energy. The way we navigated the dilemma between feasibility and vision in this book was twofold.

On the one hand we followed what you could call a process approach. We stuck to our twin concepts of complexity and hegemony. Complexity is a human predicament that cannot be willed away. Yet political, administrative and corporate institutions tend to ignore complexity and favour linear explanations and solutions to collective problems. Hegemony, as we explained in Chapter 1, is a form of cognitive captivity, in which we are unable to see beyond our cognitive, moral and practical horizon. Hegemony throws a veil over our assumptions and institutions and makes them invisible, as Unger also says. The sense the world makes, its obvious uncontested meaning, is hardwired into our very language. The moral anaesthesia that has accompanied the COVID-19 pandemic so far is a sad illustration of hegemony. Throughout the book we have tried to keep our gaze firmly on these twin predicaments.

Taking complexity seriously forces us to think of solutions holistically and in an integrative manner. It is the acknowledgement that, in an ontological sense, things hang together. For this reason we presented a series of analyses and proposals that build upon each other, and support solutions to the number one issue of our times: the looming climate catastrophe. If we learned one thing from our engagement with the climate change literature, it is that the window for effective and meaningful solutions is closing rapidly. If we cannot keep global warming within 1.5°C before 2030, our planet, and in particular the countries in the Global South, will be overwhelmed with the effects of extreme weather, rising sea levels, lethal droughts, uncontrollable wildfires and overheated cities. As we pointed out in Chapter 9, to avoid climate collapse by 2030 there is no alternative but a radical solution (Aronoff et al, 2019, 18). In that sense, creating a sustainable society is the centrepiece of our plan for a better post-COVID society.

However, as we showed, the measures needed to achieve that goal require reforms and transformations in all the areas that we discussed in this book. For example, we cannot hope to divest from carbon-based technologies and invest in sustainable production methods with the current footloose global financial system that is able to move capital in and out of countries with a few keystrokes. We urgently need capital controls. We also need a public spending programme aimed at creating jobs that care for the community, for people, and for the environment (Tcherneva, 2018, 8). And we need a government system that is up to the job and does not diminish itself by embracing untenable ideological positions. The elements of a new, better society that we described in this book are strong public and social infrastructures, good, affordable and secure housing, decent and fairly paid jobs, good government, real corporate responsibility, and a finance sector that is under democratic control. These are the conditions of possibility for effective climate policy.

In our current situation effective climate policy is, of course, an urgent instrumental achievement. We need to contain global warming before it overwhelms us. But climate policy is, above all, a reorientation of human value. This is the second way we tried to deal with the dilemma between feasibility and vision. We did not formulate a positive vision or a statement of principles at the outset because they are likely to remain empty. Valence words without urgency. You can take it or you can leave it, you can even put it on the website of your organisation, but the words do not incite you to action. The progressive-humanitarian vision of Red Vienna was not some kind of preformulated party platform. It was forged in the struggle to overcome the appalling material conditions of Vienna in the aftermath of the First World War. It was refined in a pitched battle with the communist left that wanted the imposition of a Marxist doctrine and the far right that wanted to topple the Social-Democrats altogether. Progressive humanism thus had a very concrete meaning to the politicians and officials of the city. To them it was a vibrant vision alive with possibilities. Somewhat in this spirit we wanted to show, not prescribe. We did this by alluding to values of inclusiveness, solidarity, sustainability, cooperation, connectedness, participation and mutual respect and in our analyses of problems and suggestions for solutions. And, inspired by indigenous ways of knowing, we also introduced a different, more inclusive and respectful way of interacting with the non-human world. At least the reader can see these values at work.

For example, by introducing the metaphor of gardening, we showed how we can change our relationship towards the natural environment and towards other human beings and other non-human species. A relationship that is less calculating, less exploitative, less competitive, more aimed at cooperation and community. For this reason we suggested a shift from a metaphor of human mastery, which we called the engineering paradigm, to one of modesty and collaboration and an acknowledgement of our limits – what we called the gardening paradigm. We hope that this sets in motion what George Monbiot calls the Values Ratchet (Monbiot, 2014). It means that the political environment in which we live suggests to us the values that the wider society considers important. For example, if we live in a society that takes it for granted that everyone has access to quality health care and secure housing, it becomes normal to care for strangers or to expect empathy, decency or community from our public officials and each other. Reversely, if the dominant ideology is that society is a fierce competition for survival, it makes it less likely that providing for the less fortunate is a collective duty (Monbiot, 2014; 2017, 9). The Values Ratchet is also called policy feedback, but it is obvious that the feedback is not linear. Distrust and hostility towards migrants are widespread, for example. Also, people start to take social achievements for granted, a process called entitlement. But it holds out hope that well-designed policy measures can indeed lead to a better society.

Policy feedback also applies, in a reflexive way, to the process of policy making. Much policy practice follows an implicit social engineering pattern. After the political struggle over agenda setting and problem formulation has been settled, a small, specialist group of politicians and administrators designs and implements solutions to the agreed on problem formulations. They have a limited set of so-called policy instruments available – think of budgets, taxes, subsidies, fines, rules – with which to realise policy intention. The instruments are then distributed to the field and applied by administrators. Within the discipline of policy studies there has always been an undercurrent of a different, more deliberative, kind of policy making. The thrust of deliberative policy making is to extent the dialogue between stakeholders from agenda setting to all phases of the policy process. Inclusive groups of stakeholders sit down and work together to formulate problems, pool their resources to design creative solutions, and realise these solutions in an ongoing process of intervention, monitoring of outcomes, and adjusting the development of the policy (Hajer and Wagenaar, 2003; Wagenaar, in press). In this way, the lived experience and local knowledge of stakeholders is a continuous input throughout the policy process. In Chapter 2 we saw that this way of increasing diversity within a group is one of the ways to harness complexity. Inclusiveness results in more effective and more democratic policy making.

Associations and administration: the return of developmental democracy

But how do we get there? Let's be realistic. The current political-economic constellation does not provide many reasons for optimism. As we argued in Chapter 1, the COVID-19 crisis has revealed major problems with government and business. In many countries, authoritarian tendencies are on the rise, governments are overwhelmed, fuelled by social media, polarisation within the population has increased (sometimes stoked by opportunistic political leaders), and large businesses see an opportunity to increase their power and wealth. Large parts of the population have lost their job and have descended into severe poverty. In Chapter 6 we have argued that it is time for the public sector to regain its faith in itself. Using the example of Red Vienna we have shown what a creative, assertive administration can achieve. The state must take back control over public services and allow its citizens more influence over their supply and direction.

Although we need government and business to get us out of our mess, we cannot expect them to do this on their own. The liberal democratic model that has governed the advanced economies of the West has reached its limit. Its economic externalities have caught up with it. It is in need of serious reform.

The outline of such reform would combine the legitimacy of democratic influence, the effectiveness of expert administration and the openness and creativity of associational life within civil society. It would apply these principles to *all* realms of public life. Differently put, it would break down the firewall between economy and society that is characteristic of our capitalist political economy. We need to enlarge the scope of democratic influence. Issues that are central to human flourishing, such as work and money, are brought under democratic control. In general, economic transactions are regarded as an intrinsic part of social and natural life, subject to their customs and requirements, and not a separate domain opposite and in many instances antithetical to social life. Below, we sketch the principles of what we call an *Ecological Society*.

The idea of an *Ecological Society* rests on three principles: a rich associational civil society, problem-driven practical deliberation, and the creation of intermediary structures that mediate between state agencies and associational civic life. We value *a rich associational life* for five reasons. Associations are incubators for creative solutions to pressing problems. For example, civic enterprises, groups of citizens who produce social goods and services such as green energy or social care, are skilled in organising their 'production model' in such a way that they use the same resource to attain multiple goals (Wagenaar, 2019; van der Heijden and de Blok, 2020). Second, they teach citizens the skills that are needed to solve problems together. Think of mundane skills such as chairing a meeting, drawing up minutes, managing a budget, but also complex skills such as conflict resolution, or creating and maintaining partnerships with government agencies. Third, one of the skills central to associations is deliberation. Citizens employ a kind of democratic etiquette in their interactions with each other and with external actors such as politicians (Wagenaar, 2007). This does not mean, of course, that social movements cannot use more confrontational methods to draw attention to an important cause.

Fourth, civic associations are schools of democracy where citizens learn about collective problems, the information and knowledge needed to understand and solve them, and the values that sustain democracy. The benefits of associations are that they enable individuals to achieve objectives they cannot achieve on their own and that they contribute to personal development. As the late Paul Hirst, one of the great theorists of associative democracy, summarises it:

> [A]ssociation – through the interaction of individuals, to them giving of themselves in service to others, and through them striving to attain some common purpose – enhances the individual both in some specific sense related to the objectives of the voluntary body in question ... and as a person, developing their capacities through running or participating in the work of the group. (1994, 50)

Associations are a form of developmental democracy – a richer form of democracy that rests on a moral vision of a better society to be achieved by citizens who interact freely and, in the process, enhance their own political capacity and that of society at large (Macpherson, 1977, 60). The importance of asserting the practical and moral importance of developmental democracy once again is that it has been all but vitiated in the 20th century by the market model of electoral liberal democracy in which politicians compete for the vote and citizens select the candidate that fits their interests (Macpherson, 1977, 76). But, as has become clear during the pandemic and in the face of the looming climate catastrophe, the externalities of thin, electoral democracy have overwhelmed us. Polarisation, authoritarian tendencies, ideologically-driven policy making, self-inflicted administrative incapacitation, and extreme wealth inequalities, are symptoms of a political system badly in need of repair. The involvement of associations in government and economy is our best hope.

Finally, civic associations fulfil a fifth function, the monitoring of power elites. As we have seen, civic associations hold governments and businesses to account and pressure them to act on unacceptable social ills and urgent problems. They influence the political agenda. Without civic associations we would not have had a divest and #keepitintheground movement. At the moment only social movements create the necessary urgency in fighting global warming. They are a key element in what the democratic theorist John Keane calls 'monitory democracy'. He describes it as a new phase in the development of democracy, 'a "post-parliamentary" politics defined by the rapid growth of many different kinds of extra-parliamentary, power-scrutinising mechanisms' (2009, 688).

One of the strengths of associations is their *problem-driven perspective*. As Ansell says, practical problems 'pin disputes about knowledge, principles, and values down to particulars ... and they focus our attention on action and consequences' (2011, 11). It is a well-known principle of casuistry that people who disagree about abstract principles find it easier to achieve consensus when those principles are embodied in a concrete case. The problem-driven perspective is built into the organisation structures of civic associations. They exist to address pressing societal and environmental issues that individuals on their own cannot solve. This is what makes them ideal partners for public agencies. These have the reputation of being sluggish, bureaucratic and inward-looking, and some of them certainly are. But public agencies work in the frontline of societal dislocation. They deal with concrete problems and people. They are the last line of defence. They can decide not to address a particular issue, but they cannot walk away from it. This is why public agencies and the administrators working there are often open to pragmatic, non-ideological solutions, in cooperating to solve problems. Civic associations often reach parts of the community that are closed to government agencies. On the other hand, the latter have the means and democratic legitimacy to see through decisions and distribute workable solutions over a much wider territory than local associations.

Civic associations by themselves do not have the power to govern society. They are too fragmented, too local, and they often lack the resources. To realise a decision or a solution, an organisation needs resources (money, information tools) and the democratic legitimacy to get people to accept its requirements or demands. For this reason, we concluded earlier that we cannot get around the state and businesses in transforming our current dysfunctional political economy. But states have ideologically incapacitated themselves and large corporations live under the dictate of maximising shareholder value. We need *intermediary structures*. Intermediary structures mutually connect public administration and business on one hand and associations on the other. This, admittedly, is one of the most difficult and least developed elements of democratic theory.

In areas such a policing, education and habitat conservation, states have begun to experiment with the devolution of problem solving to local associations (Fung and Wright, 2003). The advantages over uniform, centralised policy making is that the local organisations act on their intimate, hands-on knowledge of local circumstances, have the trust of citizens, and are often more flexible to adapt to changing conditions and the backtalk of their interventions. The problem with devolution to local associations is, however, that they are at the mercy of the central authority and do not affect the operating routines of state agencies. As we saw, the strengths of associations reside in their governance structure: horizontal, inclusive, problem-oriented, deliberative. State agencies have few incentives to adopt such governance principles. They operate under the law of large numbers and therefore require standard operating routines to get the work done. They use public money and are accountable for its proper spending. Merging the operating principles of state agencies and civic associations has proven to be the philosopher's stone of democratic theory and public administration.

We do not have the space to give an overview of the experiments and solutions that figure in the literature (see Bourgon, 2011 and De Souza Briggs, 2008, for examples). Corporatist solutions give civic associations (unions, employer organisations, but also umbrella organisations in other societal domains) a place at the table to deliberate on policy proposals. The government uses the outcome of the deliberations in its decision making. The implementation of those decisions is left to state agencies. This traditional model has been adapted to contemporary developments. For example, the over 1,500 citizen care initiatives that have emerged in the Netherlands over the past decade are represented by an umbrella organisation that now has a voice in national policy making (NLZVE, 2020). A second class of solutions aims at merging state and civil society in policy making and implementation. The classic example is the Porto Alegre participatory budgeting initiative. The initiative cleverly merged decentralised political decision making and centralised coordination so that the city budget was representative of the priorities of the city districts and larger interests of the city. Participatory budgeting has been widely implemented across the world, often in watered down versions. The singular success of the Porte Alegre initiative seems to depend on the city's unique political makeup (Avritzer, 2009). A third approach is to infuse public administration with large doses of deliberation. This approach is promising as it has proven to be able to resolve policy impasse and conflict, and generate creative solutions for difficult, evolving policy problems (Innes and Booher, 2010; Forester, 2009; Curato et al, 2017). We argue that the design and development of intermediary structures should be one of the spearheads of democratic, policy and administrative theory in the coming years.

Reimagining society

What the example of Red Vienna taught us is the importance of an overarching vision. Without such a vision, efforts at policy change and institutional reform run the risk of remaining stuck within the local confines where they usually originate. Also, an appealing vision helps reforms to take root by anchoring them in the value structure of the wider culture. As Ruth Levitas (2013, 153) argued, a utopian vision projects images of the good society and the kind of people such societies develop and encourage. Red Vienna's progressive humanist vision was effective because it was 'double-edged'. On the one hand it was rooted in abstract values such as solidarity, social justice and self-actualisation, as well as a pedagogical approach to progressive policy making, while on the other it was always aimed at the realisation of these values in concrete situations. Such an actionable vision has various functions. It helps actors to make sense of the chaotic stream of events and occurrences that always threaten to overwhelm them. But it also makes possible a kind of 'design-in-practice', a flexible, yet guided, response to the confusing dialectic of intervention and backtalk. A broad, open-ended but actionable vision has generative properties. By constantly linking concrete problems to the meta-concepts of the larger vision, both are developed and extended (Ansell, 2011, 54). These visions are 'constructively ambiguous'. They provide a 'soft teleology that invokes an emotional response', thereby giving direction to cooperative political ventures (Ansell, 2011, 56).

We concluded the preceding chapter with the observation that we live in the age of the Anthropocene (Pálsson, 2020) and that we believe that humankind's negative impact on the Earth that this concept encapsulates can be turned around. The concept of *Ecological Society* that we introduced here is perhaps the kernel of such a positive transformation. The book provides the necessary building blocks to realise our vision of an *Ecological Society*. We described beliefs, values and practices in all the domains that are conditions for a flourishing society; flourishing that is for humankind and the Earth. In doing this we tried to overcome the hegemonic hold that a neoliberal, anti-democratic ideology has on our collective consciousness and individual beliefs. We also tried to respect the complex nature of our world that dictates that every attempt at collective problem solving must be integrative. We hope that this short book will help us imagine, and above all realise, an *Ecological Society*.

Notes

Chapter 1

[1] https://wolfstreet.com/2021/02/09/when-the-eviction-bans-end-how-many-more-renters-face-eviction-than-in-good-times-how-much-worse-is-it-now/.

Chapter 3

[1] We focus on Dewey, but those who are interested in the importance of pragmatism for economic, political and democratic transformation could do worse than read the work of Mary Parker Follett. While for most of the 20th century she was one of the invisible women of American philosophy, she has been rediscovered recently as one of the most important theorists of participatory democracy and organisational reform. She was also a major feminist thinker (Follett, 1998 [1918]; Whipps, 2014; Stout and Love, 2015).

[2] Pragmatism's penchant for experimentation as a strategy for practical institutional reform has important similarities with the democratic experimentalism of the Brazilian philosopher Robert Unger. Unger's is probably the most elaborate and integrated contemporary utopian alternative to market capitalism and social democracy. He attempts to restore the broken link between conditions of practical progress and the needs and aspirations of ordinary men and women (Unger, 1998, 10). This vision informs the practice of a 'motivated, sustained and cumulative tinkering with the arrangements of society' (Unger, 1998, 16). Unger's book is an intricate and wide-ranging attempt to put this program into practice one that breaks free from the North-Atlantic hegemony in political theory and practice.

Chapter 4

[1] This narrative culminated in the obliteration of any reference to democracy in George W. Bush's ideal of an 'ownership society' in his 2004 election campaign (Ron, 2008, 186). Apart from individual home ownership, the ownership society also included privatised retirement and health savings accounts, tuition loans and school vouchers. In Chapter 6 we will discuss the intellectual soil in which these ideas and practices took root.

[2] Aalbers (2016, 2) defines the term financialisation as follows: 'the increasing dominance of financial actors, markets, practices, measurements and narratives, at various scales, resulting in a structural transformation of economies, firms (including financial institutions), states and households. Financialization thus describes the growing interdependence of economic actors at all levels through the mechanism of financial markets' (Aalbers, 2016, 2).

[3] Total household debt in Great Britain was £1.28 trillion in April 2016 to March 2018, of which £119 billion (9 per cent) was financial debt and £1.16 trillion (91 per cent) was property debt. Total household financial debt rose by £12 billion (11 per cent) in the latest period, up from £107 billion in April 2014 to March 2016. A lot of the increase was in student debt and so called 'hire purchase debt'. The latter are loans to buy consumer goods that the customer only owns once the last payment has been made (Kidd, 2019).

[4] There is also evidence that, in the domain of housing, the property-owning democracy does not attain its goal of furthering the democratic involvement of

property owners in deliberative involvement in community affairs. In a study on home ownership and democratic involvement, Lundqvist (1998, 231) concludes, 'home owners as a group do not stand out as examples of civility and democratic spirit compared to citizens in other housing tenures'.

Chapter 6

[1] Foucault has done this himself of course with his lectures on governmentality. Nikolas Rose (2012) has moved Foucault's genealogy of governing in the liberal state into the present. But both restricted themselves to political ideas and did not include the influence of the political economy on the collective understanding of and expectations about government. The edited volume by Mirowski and Plehwe, *The Road from Mont Pèlerin* (2015), relates the story of the development of the current neoliberal discourse about the economy but has little to say about its effect on the collective conception of government.

[2] The national settlements between capital and labour are only part of the story of the development of the postwar welfare state. In fact, it was the Bretton Woods system, negotiated among the Allies in 1944, that established an international financial architecture that reined in the speculative power of finance and created the conditions for mixed economies in the spirit of the New Deal (Kuttner, 2018, xiv). Bretton Woods was imperfect, but it allowed the precarious balance between the monetary requirements for international trade and the existence needs of workers in domestic economies (Rodrik, 2012).

[3] For purposes of symmetry Streeck uses the term 'market justice', which he describes as the 'distribution of the output of production according to the market evaluation of individual performance, expressed in relative prices; the yardstick for remuneration according to market justice is marginal productivity, the market value of the last unit of output under competitive conditions' (2017, 58). With this overly cumbersome definition Streeck no doubt wants to emphasise the quasi-exactness of the assessment of market justice.

Chapter 7

[1] The figures for Europe are more mixed. In the Mediterranean and German-speaking countries, SMEs make up a larger percentage of all businesses and employ more people than in the Netherlands or the UK. Germany has 'exported' many SMEs to central European countries as suppliers to its care industry. Overall, in Europe, two out of three employees work in an SME, and SMEs are the main drivers of job creation (OECD, 2019).

[2] At the 2016 Conservative party conference, former UK prime minister Theresa May said: 'If you believe you are a citizen of the world, you are a citizen of nowhere.' Her words immediately drew controversy. She was criticised for endorsing nativism and being hostile to cosmopolitanism. Some critics pointed out similarities to a speech by the leader of the German extremist right, some would say fascist, party *Alternative für Deutschland* (Alternative for Germany, AfD), and even detected shades of Hitler's language.

[3] And through charity. As Linsey McGoey showed in her influential book *No Such Thing as a Free Gift* (2015), philanthropies do not only crowd out democratically legitimised and publicly accountable authorities and organisations from funding policy measures, but they also determine policy agendas.

Chapter 8

[1] Central banks also create central bank reserve money, which we shall return to later. As this does not circulate in the economy, we do not include it in our discussion of the money supply (Ryan-Collins et al, 2011).

[2] The multiplier effect offsets some of the calculation. The lender will use the money to make it work in the real economy thereby adding to GDP. For example, by buying a house, we will likely spend money on renovation and furnishing the house, thereby supporting contractors, plumbers, kitchen and furniture stores and so on.

[3] In a report issued by the Federal Bank of New York that outlines seven 'frictions' in the securitisation of mortgages, almost all of them stem from information asymmetries between the different parties. For example, 'The originator has an information advantage over the arranger with regard to the quality of the borrower.' And: 'The arranger has more information about the quality of the mortgage loans which creates an adverse selection problem: the arranger can securitise bad loans (the lemons) and keep the good ones. This third friction in the securitisation of subprime loans affects the relationship that the arranger has with the warehouse lender, the credit rating agency (CRA), and the asset manager.' Or 'The rating agencies are paid by the arranger and not investors for their opinion, which creates a potential conflict of interest. The opinion is arrived at in part through the use of models (about which the rating agency naturally knows more than the investor) which are susceptible to both honest and dishonest errors.' (Ashcraft and Schuermann, 2008, i–ii) In plain English, this is called deception.

[4] Rehypothecation is the re-use of collateral for multiple loans, thereby progressively weakening the collateral. Shadow banks use this practice to increase the amount of credit they issue (Brown, 2019, 73). The 'Safe Harbor clause' was passed by US Congress in 2005, after much lobbying from Wall Street, and stipulates that collateral posted by bankrupt borrowers for repo loans and derivatives is exempt from bankruptcy proceedings. Some analysts blame the safe harbour clause for the collapse of Lehman Brothers. When the bank was in trouble, the repo and derivatives traders rushed in to claim their collateral and the bank instantly went illiquid (Brown, 2019, 80). Bail-in means that a bankrupt bank, instead of going through bankruptcy proceedings, can, under certain conditions, confiscate bondholder's money to recapitalise itself (Brown, 2019, 99). These bonds are called 'contingent capital convertible instruments' (CoCo Bonds). For reasons of system risk, (shadow) banks are prohibited from buying these CoCo bonds; most of them end up in the portfolios of pension funds. We cannot resist quoting an indignant financial analyst on bail-in. With bail-in 'the order of creditor seniority is changed. (in case of bankruptcy). ... The cronies (other banks and government) ... get 100 percent or more; the non-cronies, including non-interest bearing depositors who should be super-senior, get a kick in the guts instead ...' (Brown, 2019, 100).

[5] Handbag economics is a classic case of what the sociologist Linsey McGoey would call 'strategic ignorance'. Strategic ignorance is not a lack but a resource, she says, that enables 'knowledge to be deflected, obscured, concealed or magnified in a way that increases the scope of what remains unintelligible' (McGoey, 2019).

[6] Critics of MMT point out that injecting money in the nongovernment sector through government deficits will result in inflation. This is far too big a topic to discuss here. But let it be said that (1) empirically inflation has so far not materialised despite trillion-dollar injections of money in the finance system to bail out banks,

and (2) MMT claims that it will address inflation before it happens. In fact, MMT has both a more differentiated understanding of what causes inflation (not just excess demand) and a more varied suite of information and policy tools to address inflation before it happens (Fullwiler et al, 2019).

[7] According to the British Advocacy campaign Global Justice Now, there are now more than 3,400 trade and investment treaties and agreements that protect transnational investments. Most of these treaties overrule national law, in effect placing them outside the reach of public policy and democratic control (Pettifor, 2019, 74).

[8] This proposal is informed by Huber and Robertson (2000), as well as proposals of the Positive Money movement in the UK.

[9] Seigniorage is the profit that a money issuing entity makes from the difference between exchange value of the money and the production costs. This difference is obviously considerable in a public money system given the full exchange value carries no debt.

[10] There are various technicalities involved with the transition from privatised to public money. For those who are interested in these, we refer them to Huber and Robertson (2000).

[11] Pettifor argues that lowering central bank interest rates in effect increases real interest rates in the productive economy thereby dampening economic activity (2017, 137).

[12] In the world of international finance this is coded language for a regulatory race to the bottom. The phrase 'regulatory arbitrage' is often used by bankers to resist caps on bonuses, or higher capital requirements, and is usually accompanied by calls for a 'level playing field' (Rodrik, 2012, 314).

Chapter 9

[1] It falls outside the scope of this book to discuss the very concept of epistemology as a deep hegemonic structure that rules our institutions of science, management and education. For a brilliant discussion of this hegemonic project, see Charles Taylor's essay 'Overcoming epistemology' (1995).

[2] There is a lot of discussion about what the 'right' GND is, and what versions of it do not deserve the name – Aronoff and colleagues, for example, speak of a 'faux Green New Deal' for when the label is used to signify something far less ambitious (2019, 16). Joe Biden was one of the people who was long called out for supporting too toothless a vision for a sustainable society – in fact he refused to back anything that bore the name GND (most likely out of fear of losing support in swing states where large numbers of people worked in the carbon industry, such as Pennsylvania). Once it was clear, however, that Biden would be the Democratic Party's candidate in the presidential race, he worked with a wide range of people to develop what was to become the 'Biden Plan'. His collaborators and advisors included Varshini Prakash of the Sunrise Movement, as well as Congresswoman Ocasio-Cortez, and his former competitor Bernie Sanders (Biden, 2020) and the result was a version of the GND in all but in name. Not only did Biden vow to re-join the Paris agreement that the country left under President Trump, but in July 2020, the presidential candidate announced a $2 trillion plan to tackle climate change over the next four years. Just as with the GND, the Biden plan places a strong focus on clean energy, job creation, housing and large public infrastructure projects. It promises to create millions of new and fairly paid jobs that are intended

to support the country's transition into clean and green automobility. He also announced to build about 1.5 million new housing units and upgrade millions of homes to make them more energy efficient. Pollution from oil and gas wells as well as from coal mining sites should be cleaned up (which will create new jobs as well). By 2035, the country's power sector should be pollution free, and net-zero emissions should be reached by 2050.

Whether Biden will be able to implement any of this will depend on whether he will be able to find the necessary support in the Senate. The situation is different in Europe, where Commission President von der Leyen is a proponent of the GND. The 'Communication on the European Green Deal' (the term 'new' was omitted here), led by von der Leyen, was launched just before the beginning of the COVID-19 pandemic in December 2019. In it the European Commission announced the intention to decarbonise European economies within 30 years; a much less ambitious – or, depending on one's perspective, a much more realistic – plan than the GND plans in America.

References

Aalbers, M.B. (2016) *The Financialisation of Housing. A Political Economy Approach*, Milton Park, Abingdon: Routledge.

Ansell, C.K. (2011) *Pragmatist Democracy. Evolutionary Learning as Public Philosophy*, Oxford: Oxford University Press.

Aronoff, K., Battistoni, A., Cohen, D.A. and Riofracos, T. (2019) *A Planet to Win. Why We Need a Green New Deal*, London: Verso.

Ashcraft A.B. and Schuermann, T. (2008) *Understanding the Securitization of Subprime Mortgage Credit*, Staff Report no. 318 March 2008, New York: Federal Reserve Bank of New York.

Aubrey, T. (2015) 'Britain's dysfunctional housing market: a European comparison', *Policy Network*, 31 October, https://highpeaklibdems. org.uk/en/article/2015/1118196/britain-s-dysfunctional-housing-market-a-european-comparison.

Avritzer, L. (2009) *Participatory Institutions in Democratic Brazil*, Washington DC: Woodrow Wilson Center Press.

Axelrod, R. and Cohen, M.D. (2000) *Harnessing Complexity. Organizational Implications of a Scientific Frontier*, New York: Basic Books.

Beckett, A. (2015) 'The right to buy: the housing crisis that Thatcher built', *The Guardian*, 26 August, www.theguardian.com/society/2015/aug/26/right-to-buy-margaret-thatcher-david-cameron-housing-crisis.

van Beurden, P. and Gössling, T. (2008) 'The worth of values – A literature review on the relation between corporate social and financial performance', *Journal of Business Ethics*, 82(2): 407–424.

Biden, J. (2020) 'Biden-Sanders Unity Task Force Recommendations', https://joebiden.com/wp-content/uploads/2020/08/UNITY-TASK-FORCE-RECOMMENDATIONS.pdf.

Birchall, J. and Kettilson, L.H. (2009) *Sustainable Enterprise Programme. Resilience of the Cooperative Business Model in Times of Crisis*, Geneva: International Labour Organisation.

Blau, E. (1999) *The Architecture of Red Vienna 1919–1934*, Cambridge, MA: The MIT Press.

Booth, R. (2018) 'UK surge in housing costs for poorest "worst in western Europe"', *The Guardian*, 21 March, www.theguardian.com/society/2018/mar/21/uk-europe-housing-cost-rise-lowest-earners-report.

Bourgon, J. (2011) *A New Synthesis of Public Administration*, Montreal: McGill Queen's University Press.

Bowman, A., Ertürk, I., Folkman, P., Froud, J., Haslam, C., Johal, S., Leaver, A., Moran, M., Tsitsianis, M. and Williams, K. (2015) *What a Waste. Outsourcing and How it Goes Wrong*, Manchester: Manchester University Press.

Braun, R. (2019) *Corporate Stakeholder Responsibility. Politicizing Corporate Social Responsibility*, Budapest: Central European University Press.

Bregman, R. (2016) 'Why garbagemen should earn more than bankers', translated from Dutch by E. Manton, Evonomics, 21 April, https://evonomics.com/why-garbage-men-should-earn-more-than-bankers/.

Brown, E. (2019) *Banking on the People: Democratizing Money in the Digital Age*, Washington DC: Democracy Collaborative.

Bruder, J. (2017) *Nomadland. Surviving America in the Twenty-First Century*, New York: W.W. Norton & Company.

Brunnermeier, M. K. and Reis, R. (2019) 'A crash course on the Euro crisis', Working Paper 26229 (September), Cambridge, MA: National Bureau of Economic Research.

Bund Sozialdemokratischer AkademikerInnen (BSA) (2000b) 'Twelve theses on European financial market regulation', https://europa.bsa.at/sites/default/files/a6_brochure_financial_market.pdf.

Bund Sozialdemokratischer AkademikerInnen (BSA) (2000a) 'Banken in den Dienst der Menschen stellen. Eine Vision für eine nachhaltige Reform des Bankenwesens', www.bsa.at/sites/default/files/a6_broschre_finanzmarktgruppe_banken_in_den_dienst_der_menschen_stellen.pdf.

Cabinet Office (1999) *White Paper: Modernising Government*, March, https://webarchive.nationalarchives.gov.uk/20131205110329/http://www.archive.official-documents.co.uk/document/cm43/4310/4310-00.htm.

Caduff, C. (2020) 'What went wrong: Corona and the world after the full stop', *Medical Anthropology Quarterly*, DOI: 10.1111/maq.12599.

Camus, A. (1948) *The Plague*, translated by Stuart Gilbert, New York: Borzoi Books.

Case, A. and Deaton, A. (2020) *Deaths of Despair and the Future of Capitalism,* Princeton, NJ: Princeton University Press.

CBS – Statistics Netherlands (2020) 'Care expenditure 5.2 percent up in 2019', 11 June, www.cbs.nl/en-gb/news/2020/24/care-e xpenditure-5-2-percent-up-in-2019.

Christophers, B. (2019) 'The rentierization of the United Kingdom economy', *EPA: Economy and Space*, 0(0): 1–33, https://doi.org/10.1177/0308518X19873007.

Christophers, B. (2020) 'The PPE debacle shows what Britain is built on: rentier capitalism', *The Guardian*, 12 August, www.theguardian.com/commentisfree/2020/aug/12/ppe-britain-rentier-capitalism-assets-uk-economy.

Connolly, W.E. (2011) *A World of Becoming*, Durham, NC: Duke University Press.

Cook, S.D.N. and Wagenaar, H. (2012) 'Navigating the eternally unfolding present; toward an epistemology of practice', *American Review of Public Administration*, 42(1): 3–38.

Coote, A. and Percy, A. (2020) *The Case for Universal Basic Services*, Cambridge: Polity Press.

Cox, R.W. (1992) 'Global perestroika', in R. Miliband and L. Panitch (eds), *Socialist Register 1992: New World Order?* London: Merlin Press, 26–43.

Crewe, T. (2016) 'The strange death of municipal England', *London Review of Books*, 38(24).

Crouch, C. (2011) *The Strange Non-death of Neo-liberalism*, Hoboken, NJ: John Wiley & Sons.

Curato, N., Dryzek, J.S., Ercan,S.A., Hendriks C.M., Niemeyer, S (2017) 'Twelve key findings in deliberative democracy research', *Daedalus*, 146(3): 28–38.

Daly, H.E. (1997) *Beyond Growth. The Economics of Sustainable Development*, Boston, MA: Beacon Press.

Desjardins (2020) 'How cooperatives work', www.desjardins.com/ca/about-us/desjardins/governance-democracy/how-cooperatives-work/index.jsp.

De Souza Briggs, X. (2008) *Democracy as Problem Solving. Civic Capacity in Communities Across the Globe*, Cambridge, MA: MIT Press.

Dorling, D. (2015) *Injustice: Why Social Inequality Still Persists*, Bristol: Policy Press.

Dryzek, J.S. (1996) *Democracy in Capitalist Times. Ideals, Limits, and Struggles*, Oxford: Oxford University Press.

Economic Policy Institute (EPI) (2019) 'The productivity-pay gap', www.epi.org/productivity-pay-gap/.

Edelenbos, J. and van Meerkerk, I. (2016) 'Introduction: Three perspectives on interactive governance', in J. Edelenbos and I. van Meerkerk (eds), *Critical Reflections on Interactive Governance, Self-organization and Participation in Public Governance*, Cheltenham: Edward Elgar, 1–29.

Edwards, M. (2014) *Civil Society* (3rd edition), Cambridge: Polity Press.

European Commission (EC) (2020) 'Public Opinion', statistical online tool, https://ec.europa.eu/commfrontoffice/publicopinion/index.cfm/Chart/getChart/chartType/lineChart//themeKy/45/groupKy/226/savFile/10000.

European Group on Ethics in Science and New Technologies (EGE) (2018) 'Future of Work, Future of Society', Opinion No. 30, 19 December, Brussels, https://ec.europa.eu/info/sites/info/files/research_and_innovation/ege/ege_future-of-work_opinion_122018.pdf.

Evans, S.M. and Boyte, H.C. (1986) *Free Spaces. The Sources of Democratic Change in America*, New York: Harper & Row.

Fitzpatrick, S., Pawson, H., Bramley, G., Wood, J., Watts, B., Stephens, M. and Blenkinsopp, J. (2019) *The Homelessness Monitor. England 2019*, London: Crisis.

Follett, M.P. (1998 [1918]) *The New State. Group Organization the Solution of Popular Government*, University Park, PA: The Pennsylvania State University Press.

Forester, J. (2009) *Dealing with Differences. Dramas of Mediating Public Disputes*, Oxford: Oxford University Press.

Freeman, R. (2021) *Doing Politics*. CC BY-NC 4.0. https://doingpolitics.space/about/.

Fricker, M. (2018) 'About Repo', https://repowatch.org/about-repo/.

Friedman, T.L. (2007) 'A warning from the garden', *The New York Times*, 19 January, www.nytimes.com/2007/01/19/opinion/19friedman.html?module=inline.

Fung, A. and Wright E.O. (2003) 'Thinking about empowered participatory governance', in A. Fung and E.O. Wright (eds), *Deepening Democracy. Institutional Innovations in Empowered Participatory Governance*. London: Verso, 3–45.

Fullwiler, S., Grey, R. and Tankus, N. (2019) 'An MMT response on what causes inflation', *Financial Times Alphaville*, 1 March, https://ftalphaville.ft.com/2019/03/01/1551434402000/An-MMT-response-on-what-causes-inflation/ [Article behind paywall].

Gamble, A. (1994) *The Free Economy and the Strong State: The Politics of Thatcherism*, Basingstoke: Macmillan.

Generation Green New Deal (2020) 'S1/GenGND Conversation with Nikayla Jefferson', podcast, https://podcasts.apple.com/us/podcast/s1-gengnd-conversation-with-nikayla-jefferson/id1528667640?i=1000493761693.

Gerrits, L. (2012) *Punching Clouds: An Introduction to the Complexity of Public Decision-Making*, Litchfield Park, AZ: Emergent.

Goldstein, J. (2020) *Money. The True Story of a Made-up Thing*, New York: Hachette Books.

Graeber, D. (2011) *Debt. The First 5,000 Years*, London: Melville House.

Graeber, D. (2018) *Bullshit Jobs: A Theory*, New York: Simon & Schuster.

Gray, J. (2007) *Black Mass: Apocalyptic Religion and the Death of Utopia*, New York: Farrar, Straus and Giroux.

Greenfield, P. and Weston, P. (2020) 'Banks lent £1.9tn linked to ecosystem and wildlife destruction in 2019', *The Guardian*, 28 October, www.theguardian.com/environment/2020/oct/28/banks-lent-1-9tn-linked-to-ecosystem-and-wildlife-destruction-in-2019-report-aoe.

Haagh, L. (2019) *The Case for Universal Basic Income*, New York: John Wiley & Sons.

Habermas, J. (1973) *Legitimationsprobleme im Spätkapitalismus*, Frankfurt am Main: Suhrkamp.

Hall, P.A. and Soskice, D. (2001) 'An introduction into varieties of capitalism', in P.A. Hall and D. Soskice (eds), *Varieties of Capitalism: The Institutional Foundations of Comparative Advantage*, Oxford: Oxford University Press: 1–71.

Hajer, M. and Wagenaar, H. (eds) (2003) *Deliberative Policy Analysis: Understanding Governance in the Network Society*, Cambridge University Press.

Haskins, J. (2019) 'Democrats' "Green New Deal" is a Crazy New Deal that would be a disaster for us all', *Fox News*, 7 February, www.foxnews.com/opinion/democrats-green-new-deal-is-a-crazy-new-deal-that-would-be-a-disaster-for-us-all.

Van der Heijden J. and de Blok, D. (2020) *Reinventing Multifunctionality. Innovation through Integration*, Utrecht: Netherlands Enterprise Group.

Henkel, I. (2015) 'German public opinion is caught between scapegoating Greeks and love-bombing them', LSE Blog, 21 July, http://bit.ly/1fikcsC.

Hirst, P. (1994) *Associative Democracy: New Forms of Economic and Social Governance*, Cambridge: Polity Press.

Holm, A. (2019) 'Auf zum Neubau', *Der Freitag. Die Wochenzeitung* (26), 5 July, www.freitag.de/autoren/der-freitag/auf-zum-neubau.

Hood, C. (1991) 'A public management for all seasons?' *Public Administration*, 69: 3–19.

Hood, C. and Dixon, R. (2015) *A Government That Worked Better and Cost Less? Evaluating Three Decades of Reform and Change in UK Central Government*, Oxford: Oxford University Press.

Huber, J. and Robertson, J. (2000) *Creating New Money. A Monetary Reform for the Information Age*, London: New Economics Foundation.

Hutchinson, L. (2019) ''Europe's man on the moon moment': Von der Leyen unveils EU Green Deal'. *The Parliament Magazine*, 11 December, www.theparliamentmagazine.eu/news/article/europes-man-on-the-moon-moment-von-der-leyen-unveils-eu-green-deal.

ILO and Organization for Economic Cooperation and Development (OECD) (2015) *The Labor Share in G20 Economies*. Report prepared for the G20 Employment Working Group Antalya, Turkey, 26–27 February, www.oecd.org/g20/topics/employment-and-social-policy/The-Labour-Share-in-G20-Economies.pdf.

Innes, J.E. and Booher, D.E. (2010) *Planning with Complexity. An Introduction to Collaborative Rationality for Public Policy*, Milton Park, Abingdon: Routledge.

International Labour Organization (ILO) (2016) 'Non-standard employment around the world: understanding challenges, shaping prospects', www.ilo.org/wcmsp5/groups/public/---dgreports/---dcomm/---publ/documents/publication/wcms_534326.pdf.

Jager-Vreugdenhil, M. (2012) *Nederland Participatieland? De Ambitie van de Wet maatschappelijke ondersteuning (Wmo) en de Praktijk in Buurten, Mantelzorgrelaties en Kerken*, Amsterdam: Amsterdam University Press.

Jenkins, S. (2020) 'The revolving door between City banks and Westminster is distorting our economy', *The Guardian*, 20 August, www.theguardian.com/commentisfree/2020/aug/20/politics-banking-unhealthy-whitehall-city.

Jones, C. and Murie, A. (2006) *The Right to Buy. Analysis & Evaluation of a Housing Policy*, Oxford: Blackwell Publishing.

Judt, T. (2010) *Ill Fares the Land: A Treatise on our Current Discontents*, London: Alan Lane.

Kaiser Family Foundation (KFF) (2020) 'Public opinion on single-payer, national health plans, and expanding access to medicare coverage', 16 October, www.kff.org/slideshow/public-opinion-on-single-payer-national-health-plans-and-expanding-access-to-medicare-coverage/.

Kay, J. (2015) *Other People's Money. Masters of the Universe or Servants of the People?* London: Profile Books.

Keane, J. (2009) *The Life and Death of Democracy*, London: Simon and Schuster.

Kelton, S. (2020) *The Deficit Myth. Modern Monetary Theory and How to Build a Better Economy*, London: John Murray

Kidd, C. (2019) 'Household debt in Great Britain: April 2016 to March 2018', London: Office for National Statistics, www.ons.gov.uk/peoplepopulationandcommunity/personalandhouseholdfinances/incomeandwealth/bulletins/householddebtingreatbritain/april2016tomarch2018.

Kimmerer, R.W. (2013) *Braiding Sweetgrass. Indigenous Wisdom, Scientific Knowledge and the Teaching of Plants*, London: Penguin Books.

Kittel, B., Waibel, M. and Resch, T. (2020) 'Corona, Umwelt, Klima & Nachhaltigkeit', *Vienna Center for Electoral Research*, 3 July, https://viecer.univie.ac.at/corona-blog/corona-blog-beitraege/blog63/.

Kofler, S. (2004) 'Wohnen im Karl-Marx-Hof 1930–1934. Der kurze Traum vom besseren Leben', MA thesis, University of Vienna.

Komlosy, A. (2018) *Work: The Last 1000 Years*, London: Verso Books.

Kuttner, R. (2018) *Can Democracy Survive Global Capitalism?* New York: W.W. Norton & Company.

Laville, S. (2019) 'Fossil fuel big five "spent €251m lobbying EU" since 2010', *The Guardian*, 24 October, www.theguardian.com/business/2019/oct/24/fossil-fuel-big-five-spent-251m-lobbying-european-union-2010-climate-crisis.

Levitas, R. (2013) *Utopia as Method. The Imaginary Reconstitution of Society*. Houndmills, Basingstoke: Palgrave MacMillan.

Ludwig, M. (2017) 'Das Wiener Modell – der soziale Wohnungsbau in Wien', in BDB, Bund Deutscher Baumeister, Architekten und Ingenieure e.V. (ed), *Jahrbuch 2017 mit Sachverständigenverzeichnis*, Berlin: Bund Deutsche Baumeister, Architekten und Ingenieure, e.V, 22–35, www.smartertogether.at/wp-content/uploads/2017/09/2017-02-Beitrag_Wiener-Wohnbau_BDB-Jahrbuch-2017.pdf.

Lundqvist, L.J. (1998) 'Property-owning and democracy – do the twain ever meet?', *Housing Studies*, 13(2): 217–231.

Maclean, N. (2017) *Democracy in Chains. The Deep History of the Radical Right's Stealth Plan for America,* Melbourne: Scribe.

Macpherson, C.B. (1977) *The Life and Times of Liberal Democracy*, Oxford: Oxford University Press.

Maderthaner, W. (2019) 'Das kommunale Experiment. Die "Veralltächligung" der Utopie?' in M. Schwartz, G. Spitaler and E. Widal (eds), *Das Rote Wien 1919–1934*, Basel: Birkhäuser, 24–30.

Makortoff, K. (2020) 'Covid has highlighted America's flaws, says bank boss Jamie Dimon', *The Guardian,* 5 October, www.theguardian.com/business/2020/oct/05/covid-has-highlighted-americas-flaws-says-bank-boss-jamie-dimon.

Manuel, F.E. and Manuel, F.P. (1979) *Utopian Thought in the Western World*, Cambridge, MA: Harvard University Press.

Maynard-Moody, S. and Musheno, M. (2003) *Cops, Teachers, Counselors: Stories from the Front Lines of Public Service*, Ann Arbor, MI: University of Michigan Press.

McCall, V., Satsangi, M. and Greasley-Adams, C. (2020) 'The legacy of the Right to Buy and the differentiation of older home owners', *Social Policy & Society*, 19(2): 225–241, https://doi.org/10.1017/S1474746419000320.

McGoey, L. (2015) *No Such Thing as a Free Gift. The Gates Foundation and the Price of Philanthropy*, London: Verso.

McGoey, L. (2019) *The Unknowers. How Strategic Ignorance Rules the World*, London: Zed Books.

Meek, J. (2017) 'Somerdale to Skarbimierz', *London Review of Books*, 39(8): 3–15.

Mellor, M. (2016) *Debt or Democracy. Public Money for Sustainability and Social Justice*, London: Pluto Press.

Merret, S. (1979) *State Housing in Britain*, London: Routledge & Keagan Paul.

Mirowski, P. (2014) *Never Let a Serious Crisis Go to Waste: How Neoliberalism Survived the Financial Meltdown*, London: Verso.

Mirowski, P. and Plehwe, D. (2015) *The Road from Mont Pèlerin: The Making of the Neoliberal Thought Collective* (new edition), Cambridge, MA: Harvard University Press.

Mishel, L. and Wolfe, J. (2019) 'CEO compensation has grown 940% since 1978', Washington DC: Economic Policy Institute, 14 August.

Mitchell, S. (2016) *Monopoly Power and the Decline of Small Business. The Case for restoring America's Once Robust Antitrust Policies*, Minneapolis, MN: Institute for Local Self-Reliance.

Monbiot, G. (2014) 'The values ratchet', *The Guardian*, 10 June, www.monbiot.com/2014/06/10/the-values-ratchet/

Monbiot, G. (2017) *Out of the Wreckage. A New Politics for an Age of Crisis*, London: Verso.

Nardelli, A. and Applegate, C. (2017) '8 charts that show the difference between the UK's housing market and Europe's', *Buzzfeed*, 22 February, www.buzzfeed.com/albertonardelli/8-charts-that-show-the-difference-between-the-uk-housing-mar.

Niskanen, W.A. (1971) *Bureaucracy and Representative Government*, Chicago, IL: Aldine Atherton.

O'Connor, J. (1973) *The Fiscal Crisis of the State*, New York: St. Martin's Press.

OECD (1981) 'The welfare state in crisis. An account of the Conference on Social Policies in the 1980s', Paris, 20–23 October, Paris; OECD.

OECD (2019) *OECD SME and Entrepreneurship Outlook 2019*, Paris: OECD Publishing, https://doi.org/10.1787/34907e9c-en.

Osborne, D. and Gaebler, T. (1992) *Reinventing Government. How the Entrepreneurial Spirit is Transforming the Public Sector*, Reading, MA: Addison-Wesley.

Owen, D. (2003) 'Geneology as perspicuous representation', in C.J. Heyes (ed), *The Grammar of Politics. Wittgenstein and Political Philosophy*, Ithaca, NY: Cornell University Press, 82–99.

Pálsson, G. (2020) *The Human Age. How we Created the Anthropocene Epoch and Caused the Climate Crisis*, London: Welbeck.

Pettifor, A. (2017) *The Production of Money. How to Break the Power of Bankers*, London: Verso.

Pettifor, A. (2019) *The Case for the Green New Deal*, London: Verso.

Pew Research Center (2019) 'Public trust in government: 1958–2019', 11 April, www.pewresearch.org/politics/2019/04/11/public-trust-in-government-1958-2019/.

Pew Research Center (2020) 'Increasing share of Americans favour a single government program to provide health care coverage', 29 September, www.pewresearch.org/fact-tank/2020/09/29/increasing-share-of-americans-favor-a-single-government-program-to-provide-health-care-coverage/.

Polanyi, K. (2001) *The Great Transformation: The Political and Economic Origins of Our Time*, Boston, MA: Beacon Press.

Pollan, M. (2020) 'The sickness in our food supply', *New York Review of Books*, 67(10): 4–6.

Prainsack, B. (2020a) 'The value of healthcare data: to nudge, or not?' *Policy Studies*, 41: 547–562.

Prainsack, B. (2020b) *Vom Wert des Menschen. Warum wir ein Bedingungsloses Grundeinkommen brauchen* (The Value of Humans: Why We Need a Universal Basic Income). Wien: Brandstätter.

Prainsack, B. and Buyx, A. (2018) 'The value of work: Addressing the future of work through the lens of solidarity', *bioethics*, 32(9): 585–592, https://onlinelibrary.wiley.com/doi/full/10.1111/bioe.12507.

Prescod, P. (2020) 'We need a jobs guarantee now more than ever', *Jacobinmag*, 24 June, www.jacobinmag.com/2020/06/case-for-job-guarantee-review-pavlina-tcherneva.

Purdy, J. (2019) *This Land is Our Land. The Struggle for a New Commonwealth*, Princeton, NJ: Princeton University Press.

Quammen, D. (2020) 'We made the Coronavirus epidemic', *New York Times*, 28 January, www.nytimes.com/2020/01/28/opinion/coronavirus-china.html.

Ramaswamy, V. (2008) 'Co-creating value through customers' experiences: the Nike case', *Strategy and Leadership*, 36(5): 9–14.

Raworth, K. (2017) *Doughnut Economics. Seven Ways to Think Like a 21st-Century Economist*, London: Random House.

Reyes, O. and Balanyá, B. (2016) 'Carbon welfare. How big polluters plan to profit from EU emissions trading reform', *Corporate Europe Observatory*, https://corporateeurope.org/en/climate-and-energy/2016/12/carbon-welfare.

Rodrik, D. (2012) *The Globalization Paradox: Why Global Markets, States, and Democracy Can't Coexist*, Oxford: Oxford University Press.

Ron, A. (2008) 'Visions of democracy in "property-owning democracy": Skelton to Rawls and beyond', *History of Political Thought*, 29(1): 168–187.

Rose, N. (2012) *Powers of Freedom. Reframing Political Thought*, Cambridge: Cambridge University Press.

Ryan-Collins, J., Greenham, T., Werner, R. and Jackson, A. (2012) *Where Does Money Come From? A Guide to the UK Monetary and Banking System* (2nd edition), London: New Economics Foundation.

Sanchez Bajo, C. and Roelants, B. (2013) *Capital and the Debt Trap. Learning from Cooperatives in the Global Crisis*, Basingstoke: Palgrave Macmillan.

Saxena, S.B. (2018) 'Beyond third-party monitoring post-Rana Plaza interventions', *Economic and Political Weekly*, 53(16): 16–20.

Sayer, A. (2011) *Why Things Matter to People. Social Science, Values and Ethical Life*, Cambridge: Cambridge University Press.

Schwartz, W.M., Szeless, M. and Wögenstein, L. (2007) *Ganz Unten. Die Entdeckung des Elends. Wien, Berlin, London, Paris, New York*, Vienna: Wien Museum and Christian Brandstätter Verlag.

Schwellnus, C., Kappeler, A. and Pionnier, P.-A. (2017) 'Decoupling of wages from productivity: macro-level facts', 24 January, OECD Economics Department Working Papers No. 1373, www.oecd.org/economy/growth/Decoupling-of-wages-from-productivity-Macro-level-facts.pdf.

Self, P. (1993) *Government by the Market? The Politics of Public Choice*, Basingstoke: Macmillan.

Sheard, P. (2013) 'Repeat after me: banks cannot and do not "lend out" reserves', Standard and Poor's, 13 August.

Shove, E. (2010) 'Beyond the ABC. Climate change policies and theories of social change', *Environment and Planning A*, 42: 1273–1285.

Simpson, L.B. (2014) 'Land as pedagogy: Nishnaabeg intelligence and rebellious transformation', *Decolonization: Indigeneity, Education & Society*, 3(3): 1–25.

Smyth, S., Cole, I. and Fields, D. (2020) 'From gatekeepers to gateway constructors: credit rating agencies and the financialisation of housing associations', *Critical Perspectives on Accounting*, 71 (Sept), https://doi.org/10.1016/j.cpa.2019.102093.

Spreckley, F. (1981) 'Social audit – a management tool for co-operative working', Leeds: Beechwood College Ltd.

Sterman, J.D. (2002) 'System dynamics: systems thinking and modeling for a complex world', Working Paper Series ESD-WP-2003-01.13, Cambridge, MA: Massachusetts Institute of Technology.

Stout, L. (2012) *The Shareholder Value Myth. How Putting the Shareholders First Harms Investors, Corporations and the Public*, San Francisco, CA: Berrett-Koehler Publishers.

Stout, M. and Love, J.M. (2015) *Integrative Process. Follettian Thinking from Ontology to Administration*, Anoka, MN: Process Century Press.

Streeck, W. (2017) *Buying Time. The Delayed Crisis of Democratic Capitalism* (2nd edition), London: Verso.

Szerszynski, B. (2019) 'A planetary turn for the social sciences?', in O.B. Jensen, S. Kesselring and M. Sheller (eds), *Mobilities and Complexities*, London: Routledge: 223–227.

Taylor, C. (1995). 'Overcoming epistemology', in C. Taylor, *Philosophical Arguments*, Cambridge, MA: Harvard University Press: 1–19.

Tcherneva, P.R. (2018) 'The job guarantee: design, jobs, and implementation', *Levy Economics Institute Working Paper Collection*, Working Paper No. 902, www.levyinstitute.org/pubs/wp_902.pdf.

Tcherneva, P.R. (2020) *The Case for a Job Guarantee*, Hoboken, NJ: John Wiley & Sons.

Tiftik, E. and Mahmood, K. (2020) 'Global debt monitor. COVID-19 lights a fuse', International Institute of Finance, 6 April.

Unger, R.M. (1998) *Democracy Realized. The Progressive Alternative*, London: Verso.

US Congress (2019) 'Recognizing the duty of the Federal Government to create a Green New Deal', H. Res. 109, www.congress.gov/116/bills/hres109/BILLS-116hres109ih.pdf.

Vasudevan, A. (2020) 'Berlin's rent cap offers a new way of thinking about Britain's housing crisis', *The Guardian*, 25 November, www.theguardian.com/commentisfree/2020/nov/25/berlin-rent-cap-britains-housing-crisis-home.

Wagenaar, H., (2007) 'Governance, complexity and democratic participation: how citizens and public officials harness the complexities of neighbourhood decline', *American Review of Public Administration*, 37(1): 17–50.

Wagenaar, H. (2019) 'Making sense of civic enterprise. Social innovation, participatory democracy and the administrative state', *Partecipazione e Conflitto*, 12(2): 297–324.

Wagenaar, H. (in press) 'Assessing deliberation: methodological approaches in deliberative democracy', in H. Asenbaum, N. Curato, S.A. Ercan and R.F. Mendonça (eds), *Assessing Deliberation: Methodological Approaches in Deliberative Democracy*, Oxford: Oxford University Press.

Wagenaar, H. and Healey, P. (2015) 'Interface: the transformative potential of civic enterprise', *Planning Theory and Practice*, 16(4): 557–561.

Wagenaar, H. and Wood, M. (2018) 'The precarious politics of public innovation', *Politics and Governance*, 6(1): 150–160.

Wagenaar, H. and Wenninger, F. (2020) 'Deliberative policy analysis, interconnectedness and institutional design: lessons from "Red Vienna"', *Policy Studies*, 41(4): 411–437, https://doi.org/10.1080/01442872.2020.1717456.

Wages for Housework (n.d.) 'The Campaign for Wages for Housework', poster, http://bcrw.barnard.edu/archive/workforce/Wages_for_Housework.pdf.

Warren, M.E. (2014) 'Governance-driven democratization', in S. Griggs, A.J. Norval and H. Wagenaar (eds), *Practices of Freedom. Decentered Governance, Conflict and Democratic Participation*, Cambridge: Cambridge University Press, 38–60.

Werner, R.A. (2014) 'Can banks individually create money out of nothing? – The theories and the empirical evidence', *International Review of Financial Analysis*, 36: 1–19.

Wezerek, G. and Ghodsee, K.R. (2020) 'Women's unpaid labor is worth 10,900,000,000,000', *New York Times*, 5 March, www.nytimes.com/interactive/2020/03/04/opinion/women-unpaid-labor.html.

Whipps, J. (2014) 'A pragmatist reading of Mary Parker Follett's integrative process', *Transactions of the Charles S. Peirce Society*, 50(3): 405–424.

Wildavsky, A. (1979) *Speaking Truth to Power. The Art and Craft of Policy Analysis*, Boston, MA: Little, Brown and Company.

Wilson, J.Q. (1989) *Bureaucracy. What Government Agencies Do and Why They Do It*, New York, NY: Basic Books.

Wintour, P. (2020) 'Coronavirus: who will be winners and losers in new world order?' *The Guardian*, 11 April, www.theguardian.com/world/2020/apr/11/coronavirus-who-will-be-winners-and-losers-in-new-world-order.

Wistrich, R.S. (1983) 'Karl Lueger and the ambiguities of Viennese antisemitism', *Jewish Social Studies*, 45(3/4): 251–262.

Index

References to endnotes show the page, note and chapter number (231n3ch7).

R

Rana Plaza, Dhaka 88–9
Raworth, Kate 87–8
Real Time Gross Settlement (RTGS)
 system 106–7
Red Vienna 43–4, 81, 82, 142,
 143, 149
regulatory arbitrage 122, 154n12
rehypothecation 107, 109, 153n4
rentier capitalism 39–40, 46, 47, 75,
 106, 107
repo (repurchase) market 107, 108–10
Right to Buy scheme 34, 35, 37–8
right to clean air, water and soil 137–8
Robertson, J. 99, 104, 105, 106,
 117, 118
Rodrik, Dani 67, 80, 91, 114–15, 122
Roelants, B. 55
Roosevelt, Franklin D. 131

S

'safe harbour clause' 107, 153n4
safe housing 132
Sanchez Bajo, C. 55
Saxena, Sanchita Banerjee 88–9
seigniorage 118, 154n9
shadow banks 99, 107–10, 153n4
shareholder value 89–90, 91, 93,
 96–7, 100
Shove, Elisabeth 5, 6, 18
Simpson, Leanne Betasamosake
 129–30, 136
Skelton, Noel 34
small and medium-sized enterprises
 (SMEs) 94–5, 119, 120, 121,
 138, 152n1ch7
social movements 82, 98, 147
social reform, pragmatist theory
 of 29–32
social security 70, 138
 Dutch Disability Law 69, 71
 housing guarantee 46–9
 job guarantee programmes 61–3, 138
 universal basic income 57–61, 63, 138
 universal basic services
  movement 25–6, 27–8
social transformation, utopian method
 of 18–21
soil, right to clean 137–8
stakeholder democracy 55–6, 86, 87
Sterman, John 11–12, 13, 14
Stout, Lynn 87, 90, 92
Streeck, Wolfgang 51, 68, 70, 75, 78,
 79, 152n3ch6
subsistence as a human right 57–8
Syrian refugee crisis 1
Szerszynski, Bronislaw 3, 7

T

taxes 59, 72, 76, 95, 96, 137–8
Tcherneva, Pavlina 61, 62, 138, 143
Thatcher, Margaret 34, 35, 37, 72
think tanks, right-wing 73
transnational corporations 14, 17,
 90–4, 115
 Cadbury 85–6, 88
 and decline of SMEs 94–5
 and obstacles to CSR 95, 96–7
 'triple bottom line' 87

U

unemployment 61–2
Unger, Robert 141, 151n2ch3
United Kingdom
 housing 33–41
 'Modernising Government' White
  Paper 74
 'property-owning democracy' 34–5,
  37, 41, 47, 151–2n4
 universal basic services
  movement 25–6, 27–8
United States
 attitudes to government
  intervention 65
 Bank of North Dakota 120
 Brown vs Board of Education 70
 decline of entrepreneurialism 95
 Green New Deal 131–3
 New Deal 131
 public choice theory 73
 wage stagnation 51
universal basic income (UBI) 57–61,
 63, 138
universal basic services (UBS)
 movement 25–6, 27–8
universal job guarantees 61–3, 138
'upskilling' 53, 54
utopia 10
 as method of social
  transformation 18–21
utopian thinking 10–11, 19–20, 128–9,
 141–5, 149–50
 civil society and 97, 98
 pragmatic relevance of 29–31
 of Red Vienna 44, 82, 149

V

Values Ratchet 144
Vienna
 housing 2, 33, 41–5
 Model 42
 public infrastructures 26–7
 Red Vienna 43–4, 81, 82, 142,
  143, 149